EDITOR'S LETTER

A bitter pill to swallow

Health inequalities are silencing marginalised communities, writes **SARAH DAWOOD** – and nowhere is immune

MODERN MEDICINE IS a wonderful thing. Before Edward Jenner's development of the smallpox vaccination in 1796, infectious diseases and viruses killed millions. The introduction of anaesthetic gases during surgical procedures in 1846 eliminated the excruciating pain of surgery. And before Alexander Fleming's discovery of penicillin in 1928, people died unnecessarily from cuts and grazes.

But the benefits of modern medicine are not felt equally around the world. In this issue, we explore the forgotten patients in global healthcare settings – the marginalised groups who fall through the cracks or are actively shut out of healthcare provision, then ignored or silenced when they raise concerns.

On compiling this issue, it was obvious that the treatment of women is a huge area of worry across continents.

In the UK, Martin Bright investigates the state of whistleblowing in the National Health Service. Inadequate protections and actively malicious practices by management are preventing staff and patients from speaking out about dangerous care, particularly in maternity services.

Exiled Afghan journalist Zahra Joya investigates the dire state of women's healthcare in Afghanistan, which is now virtually non-existent under the Taliban. In Somalia, Hinda Abdi Mohamoud explores how those who speak up about the horrendous practice of female genital mutilation (FGM) are punished.

We also look at inequality where gender and ethnic discrimination collide. Katie Dancey-Downs investigates the abhorrent treatment of Roma women in Slovakia and the Czech Republic – particularly the secrecy shrouding their historical subjection to forced sterilisation. Mackenzie Argent speaks to UK-based anti-racism campaigner and medical doctor Annabel Sowemimo about the insidious self-silencing of Black women in health settings for fear of being labelled as "aggressive" or "attention-seeking".

In the fog of war, one repercussion little spoken about is psychological impact. I explore the mental health issues facing children in Gaza, many of whom are left literally speechless as trauma has caused them to lose the ability to verbally communicate.

No health-themed issue would be complete without a look at the unfettered rise of health misinformation online. Mark Honigsbaum examines what it means when this rhetoric is repeated by those in positions of power, focusing on the USA's new health secretary Robert F Kennedy Jr. Meanwhile, Ella Pawlik tells the stories of those who had legitimate adverse reactions to Covid vaccines, analysing how they have been shut out of the conversation on vaccine safety.

Outside the special report we explore the rise of corruption in Greece and delve into how digital activism is being used as a tool of resistance in Myanmar. In our culture section, we feature a short story by Ariel Dorfman and anti-colonial poetry by Diane Fahey.

Just like free speech, healthcare is an indisputable human right. But for many around the globe, both these rights are being removed in conjunction with each other. Through telling their stories, this edition aims to shine a light on these injustices and – we hope – empower more people to speak up for the right to health for themselves and others. ✖

Sarah Dawood is editor at Index on Censorship

54(01):1/1|DOI:10.1177/03064220251332525

The scales are tipped against minorities

Our cover artist, who lives in exile, speaks about her work

SYRIAN-DUTCH VISUAL ARTIST Diala Brisly was brought up in Damascus.

Initially, she created art for her own enjoyment but eventually sent some of her 2D animation work to Syria's Spacetoon children's TV channel.

Brisly's work focuses on themes of justice, psychology and wellbeing. Her illustration here depicts inequality in the global healthcare system.

She lives in exile in Amsterdam after being blacklisted during the dictatorship of Bashar al-Assad for being involved in preparing field hospitals – temporary medical facilities set up for emergencies.

Will she return home? "I don't know," she said. "Bashar al-Assad fell, but Syria isn't liberated yet."
You can see more of Brisly's work at **instagram.com/dialabrisly**

CONTENTS

Up Front

1   **A BITTER PILL TO SWALLOW:**
    SARAH DAWOOD
    Not all healthcare is made equal, and pointing this out can have serious consequences

6   **THE INDEX:** MARK STIMPSON
    From elections in Romania to breaking encryption in the UK: a tour of the world's most pressing free expression issues

Features

12 **RAPE, REPUTATION AND LITTLE RECOURSE:** SAMRIDHI KAPOOR, HANAN ZAFFAR
    Indian universities have a sexual violence problem that no one is talking about

15 **GEORGIAN NIGHTMARE:**
    RUTH GREEN
    Russian-style laws are shutting down more conversations in Georgia, with academia feeling the heat

18 **BOTSWANA'S NEW ERA:**
    CLEMENCE MANYUKWE
    From brave lawyer to president – could the country's new leader put human rights front and centre?

21 **VENEZUELA'S PRISON PROBLEM:** CATHERINE ELLIS
    The disputed new president has a way of dealing with critics – locking them up

24 **FORBIDDEN WORDS:**
    SALIL TRIPATHI
    The Satanic Verses is back in India's bookshops. Or is it?

26 **THE ART OF RESISTANCE:**
    ALESSANDRA BAJEC
    A film, a graffiti archive and a stage play: three works changing the narrative in Tunisia

29 **A TRAGIC RENAISSANCE:**
    EMILY COUCH
    The pen is getting mightier and mightier in Ukraine

32 **IN THE RED ZONE:**
    ALEXANDRA DOMENECH
    Conscription is just one of the fears of an LGBTQ+ visual artist in Russia

34 **DEMOKRATIA DISMANTLED:**
    GEORGIOS SAMARAS
    The legacy of the Predator spyware scandal has left a dark stain on Greece

36 **ELON MUSK'S YEAR ON X:**
    MARK STIMPSON
    The biggest mystery about Musk: when does he sleep?

40 **KEYBOARD WARRIORS:** LAURA O'CONNOR
A band of women are fighting oppression in Myanmar through digital activism

43 **BEHIND THE BARS OF SAYDNAYA PRISON:** LAURA SILVIA BATTAGLIA
Unspeakable horrors unfolded at Syria's most notorious prison, and now its survivors tell their stories

46 **PAINTING A TRUER PICTURE:** NATALIE SKOWLUND
Street art in one Colombian city has been sanitised beyond recognition

49 **THE REPORTING BLACK HOLE:** FASIL AREGAY
Ethiopian journalists are allowed to report on new street lights, and little else

Special Report: The forgotten patients

LOST VOICES IN THE GLOBAL HEALTHCARE SYSTEM

52 **WHISTLEBLOWING IN AN EMPTY ROOM:** MARTIN BRIGHT
Failures in England's maternity services are shrouded in secrecy

58 **AN EPIDEMIC OF CORRUPTION:** DANSON KAHYANA
The Ugandan healthcare system is on its knees, but what does that matter to the rich and powerful?

Corrections and clarifications

The following correction relates to Index Vol.53 No.4

P.30 In Ian Wylie's article Editor in Exile, the Exile Hub is an independent organisation in Thailand, not an arm of the German non-profit Media in Cooperation and Transition

CREDIT: Diala Brisly

60 **LEFT SPEECHLESS:** SARAH DAWOOD
The horrors of war are leaving children in Gaza unable to speak

64 **SPEAKING UP TO END THE CUT:** HINDA ABDI MOHAMOUD
In Somalia, fighting against female genital mutilation comes at a high price

66 **DOCTORS UNDER ATTACK:** KAYA GENÇ
Turkey's president is politicising healthcare, and medics are in the crosshairs

69 **DENIAL OF HEALTHCARE IS CENSORING POLITICAL PRISONERS – OFTEN PERMANENTLY:** RISHABH JAIN, ALEXANDRA DOMENECH, DANSON KAHYANA
Another page in the authoritarian playbook: deny medical treatment to jailed dissidents

72 **THE SILENT KILLER:** MACKENZIE ARGENT
A hurdle for many people using the UK's National Health Service: institutional racism

75 **CZECHOSLOVAKIA'S HAUNTING LEGACY:** KATIE DANCEY-DOWNS
Roma women went into hospitals to give birth, and came out infertile

78 **AN INCONVENIENT TRUTH:** ELLA PAWLIK
While Covid vaccines saved millions of lives, those with adverse reactions have been ignored

81 **PUNISHED FOR RAISING STANDARDS:** ESTHER ADEPETUN
From misuse of money to misdirecting medicines, Nigerian healthcare is rife with corruption

84 **NOWHERE TO TURN:** ZAHRA JOYA
Life as they know it has been destroyed for women in Afghanistan, and healthcare provision is no different

87 **EMERGENCY IN THE CHILDREN'S WARD:** SHAYLIM CASTRO VALDERRAMA
The last thing parents of sick children expect is threats from militia

Comment

90 **WE NEED TO TALK ABOUT SUDAN:** YASSMIN ABDEL-MAGIED
Would "a battle of narratives" give the war more attention?

92 **RFK JR COULD BE A DISASTER FOR AMERICAN HEALTHCARE:** MARK HONIGSBAUM
An anti-vaxxer has got US lives in his hands

94 **THE DIAMOND AGE OF DEATH THREATS:** JEMIMAH STEINFELD
When violent behaviour becomes business as usual

96 **FREE SPEECH V THE RIGHT TO A FAIR TRIAL:** GILL PHILLIPS
Are contempt of court laws fit for the digital age?

Culture

100 **AN UNJUST TRIAL:** ARIEL DORFMAN
A new short story imagines a kangaroo court of nightmares, where victims become defendants

107 **REMEMBER THE PAST TO SAVE THE FUTURE:** SARAH DAWOOD, DIANE FAHEY
Published exclusively, the issues of antisemitism and colonialism are recorded through poetry

110 **WHERE IT'S MORE DANGEROUS TO CARRY A CAMERA THAN A GUN:** ANTONIA LANGFORD
A singer meets filmmakers in Yemen, and both take risks to tell her story

112 **THE FIGHT FOR CHANGE ISN'T STRAIGHTFORWARD:** SHANI DHANDA
The Last Word, on exclusion and intersectional discrimination

INDEXONCENSORSHIP.ORG

CHIEF EXECUTIVE
Jemimah Steinfeld
EDITOR
Sarah Dawood
ASSISTANT EDITOR
Katie Dancey-Downs
EDITOR-AT-LARGE
Martin Bright
ASSOCIATE EDITOR
Mark Stimpson
ART DIRECTOR
Matthew Hasteley
EDITORIAL ASSISTANT
Mackenzie Argent
SUB EDITORS
Adam Aiken, Tracey Bagshaw, Sally Gimson, Jan Fox
CONTRIBUTING EDITORS
Kaya Genç, Emily Couch, Danson Kahyana, Salil Tripathi
HEAD OF POLICY & CAMPAIGNS
Jessica Ní Mhainín
POLICY & CAMPAIGNS OFFICER
Nik Williams
DEVELOPMENT OFFICER
Anna Millward
COMMUNICATIONS & EVENTS MANAGER
Georgia Beeston
CASE COORDINATOR
Daisy Ruddock
DIRECTORS & TRUSTEES
Trevor Phillips (Chair), Kate Maltby (Vice Chair), Andrew Franklin, Helen Mountfield, Elaine Potter, Mark Stephens, Nick Timothy, Ian Rosenblatt
FOUNDING EDITOR
Michael Scammell
PATRONS
Margaret Atwood, Simon Callow, Steve Coogan, Brian Eno, Christopher Hird, Jude Kelly, Matthew Parris, Alexandra Pringle, Gabrielle Rifkind, Sir Tom Stoppard, Lady Sue Woodford Hollick
ADVISORY COMMITTEE
Julian Baggini, Jeff Wasserstrom, Emma Briant, Ariel Dorfman, Michael Foley, Conor Gearty, AC Grayling, Lyndsay Griffiths, William Horsley, Anthony Hudson, Natalia Koliada, Jane Kramer, Jean-Paul Marthoz, Robert McCrum, Rebecca MacKinnon, Beatrice Mtetwa, Julian Petley, Sigrid Rausing, Kamila Shamsie, Michael Smyth, Tess Woodcraft, Christie Watson

The Index

A round-up of events in the world of free expression from Index's unparalleled network of writers and activists

Edited by
MARK STIMPSON

54(01):4/10|DOI:10.1177/03064220251332526

PICTURED: After the fall of Bashar al-Assad's regime in Syria in December, people gathered at the infamous Saydnaya prison in Damascus in a desperate search for their loved ones. The prison, known as the human slaughterhouse, saw at least 30,000 extrajudicial killings between 2011 and 2018

The Index

LEFT TO RIGHT: Georgescu and Tusk face pressure in the upcoming elections, while Tchiani dodges democracy

ELECTION WATCH

As spring rolls around, we take a look at who is – and isn't – heading to the polls

1. Romania

4-18 MAY 2025

The first round of the Romanian presidential election has actually already happened once, on 24 November 2024. A shock victory for far-right, pro-Russia independent candidate Călin Georgescu due to a strong social media campaign set up a run-off with centre-right Elena Lasconi of the Save Romania Union – or at least it would have if not for declassified intelligence documents detailing how Georgescu's meteoric rise was likely due to his campaign being pushed by a "state actor", implied to be Russia. As a result of these documents, the election result was annulled and the run-off scrapped, a decision that led to protests in the streets and incumbent president Klaus Iohannis resigning under threat of impeachment on 10 February. This ordeal left Georgescu in pole position to secure an unprecedented victory, until 26 February when he was detained by police while on his way to register for the May elections. He now faces a criminal investigation for "incitement to actions against the constitutional order", among other charges including supporting fascist groups. Raids on his associates have reportedly turned up large sums of cash and weapons, and on 9 March he was banned from running by Romania's election bureau. However, Georgescu has decided to challenge this decision, leaving Romania's future up in the air.

2. Poland

18 MAY-1 JUNE 2025

This presidential election is huge for the Polish prime minister, Donald Tusk. Despite his political alliance Civic Coalition (KO) holding power since 2023, Tusk has seen key legislation blocked by president Andrzej Duda, who is allied with the right-wing Law and Justice (PiS) party. The Polish president is largely a ceremonial role but Duda has proven to be a thorn in the side of Tusk, and this election will be a watershed moment in his second term as prime minister. As Duda is ineligible for re-election having already served two terms, the presidency is up for grabs, with both KO and PiS pushing their candidates – Warsaw mayor Rafał Trzaskowski is running for KO while PiS has nominated historian Karol Nawrocki, despite him not being a party member. With Trzaskowski leading in the polls, this could be an opportunity for Tusk and his coalition to cement their power for years to come.

3. Niger

POSTPONED – FIVE YEARS FROM NOW?

On 26 July 2023, a coup in Niger overthrew former president Mohamed Bazoum. It was the fifth such military coup since the West African nation declared independence from France in 1960. Gen Abdourahamane Tchiani, former commander of Bazoum's presidential guard, declared himself as leader of the new military junta, and proposed a three-year transition back to democracy. However, on 20 February, this promise was walked back, and the transition period was extended to five years from now, leaving Niger's future uncertain. Following the coup, Mali and Burkina Faso – both also run by military juntas – joined Niger in leaving the main regional bloc of West Africa, Ecowas, following sanctions by the bloc and demands for Niger to return to democracy. Together, they formed the Alliance of Sahel States and have made moves to distance themselves from European interference and align themselves with Russia, which is supplying them with weapons and mercenaries as they battle against terrorism in Africa's Sahel region. With a Russian embassy set to open in Niger by 2026, its political future will likely be opposed to its West African neighbours, whether or not democracy returns. ✖

MY INSPIRATION

"We're Going on a Communist Hunt"

MICHAEL ROSEN, the author of more than 200 books, including Many Different Kinds of Love: A Story of Life, Death and the NHS and the classic children's book We're Going on a Bear Hunt, writes about his parents

AS I WAS growing up, I had a sense from my parents that they weren't much like the adults I met as teachers or my friends' parents. They had stories and ways of talking that were different. My parents talked about how, when they were children, there were people on shop corners who might attack them, and how there was someone called Oswald Mosley who wanted to march at the head of some men in uniform right through where they lived. They talked of a great day when they went out to stop Mosley.

They also talked of people being prevented from working on account of who they were or what they believed, whether that was in Nazi Germany, the USA or here. Names floated in and out of our flat that seemed to have a particular flavour, like Joseph McCarthy (and "McCarthyism"), and there were stories about Paul Robeson or Pete Seeger who had been prevented from doing things. There was even a story that my father had not been able to get promotion on account of him having been a communist. Was that true, I wondered?

Then, some years later, I was encouraged to leave a traineeship at the BBC. Some time after that, a journalist came to my house and told me that this was because there had been a policy at the time (late 60s/early 70s) to not give jobs to people who they regarded as "subversive". After the journalist's visit, the story of six people (including me) was written up in a big double page spread in The Observer.

I look back over my time then and wonder what it was that I had done that had been so threatening. One story that I remember was that I was asked to make a documentary for Schools TV about biological and chemical warfare. We used footage that had already been shot and re-edited. One piece we used was of a US Army experiment in which they gave LSD to their own troops to see what happened. The result was chaos. One man was shown with his jacket buttoned up wrong and he was too befuddled to be able to button it up properly. We included this scene. After it went out, we received a letter from the US Embassy asking that we remove it. This matter was now out of my hands – I was a trainee, remember. That footage was removed.

Funnily enough, you can go online now, and there is footage of the same experiments going on with soldiers in other countries, too. ✖

Michael Rosen is currently on tour with his show Getting Through It. More details at michaelrosen.co.uk

Free speech in numbers

82 ...and counting. The number of executive orders issued by US president Donald Trump since taking office in January (correct as of 8 March)

47 The number of press associations which have condemned the decision by Trump to restrict AP's access to White House briefings after it refused to rename the Gulf of Mexico in its style guide

40 The number of Uyghurs deported by Thailand to China in February 2025

0.3% Level of overseas aid (percentage of gross national income) that the UK will give in 2027 following the government's announcement of a boost to defence spending

79% of respondents to a University of Oxford survey believe that online incitements to violence should be removed from social media platforms

RIGHT: Getting Through It is a powerful and personal double bill of monologue and poetry that delves deep into the themes of trauma, grief and mortality

The Index

PEOPLE WATCH

MACKENZIE ARGENT highlights the stories of human rights defenders under attack

Sharifeh Mohammadi
IRAN

Sharifeh Mohammadi is an Iranian human rights defender who has fought for women's rights and labour rights in Iran, and has also been a prominent voice against the death penalty. She was herself issued with the death penalty for the crime of *baghi*, "rebelling against the just Islamic ruler(s)" for peaceful human rights activities. This ruling was overturned in October 2024 by the Iranian supreme court, but the Rasht Revolutionary court reimposed her death sentence on 13 February.

Hussam Abu Safiya
PALESTINE

Palestinian paediatrician Dr Hussam Abu Safiya was the director of Kamal Adwan Hospital in northern Gaza – one of the last remaining hospitals in the region before it was evacuated, bombed and destroyed by the Israel Defense Forces in December 2024. Safiya was detained during the evacuation and has been held in arbitrary detention since. His lawyer met him in prison on 11 February and recorded a detailed statement regarding his inhumane treatment while in Ofer prison.

Dinko Gruhonjić
SERBIA

Dinko Gruhonjić is a Serbian journalist and recipient of the Weimar Prize for Human Rights, which he received for "his courageous engagement for media freedom and his critical reporting on the strengthening of militant nationalism and the glorification of war crimes in Serbia". Gruhonjić and his family have been on the receiving end of threats for years, with his reporting having drawn the ire of Serbian nationalists. These include having graffiti sprayed on his home and receiving death threats.

Mzia Amaglobeli
GEORGIA

Georgian journalist Mzia Amaglobeli, founder of local Batumi news website Batumelebi and national news site Netgazeti, was detained on 12 January for allegedly "lightly slapping" a police chief at a protest in Batumi and went on hunger strike in jail for 38 days. Amaglobeli's lawyers have alleged that the police chief verbally abused her, spat in her face and denied her access to water for several hours. She remains in detention, and if found guilty of assault she faces up to seven years in jail.

Ink spot

IN FEBRUARY, A drawn-out case against a Turkish cartoonist was postponed yet again.

Zehra Ömeroğlu is facing charges of criminal obscenity for a cartoon she drew that was published in Turkish satirical magazine LeMan in 2020. Her next hearing, the 13th in the case, is now set for 26 June.

The cartoon showed a man sniffing a partially clothed woman's bottom and saying, "At least I didn't lose my taste and smell…", referring to common symptoms of Covid.

Turkey's Board for the Protection of Minors said the cartoon violated Article 226 of the Turkish Penal Code No 5237 and said "[the cartoon's] main purpose … completely contrary to the customs, traditions and moral understanding of our society … is to create sexual arousal in the viewer and thereby profit from this".

A coalition of organisations, including Cartoonists Rights Network International, considers the findings "biased and sexist". The Coalition asked: "Would the same cartoon, published under the same circumstances, have attracted the same judicial action and censorious ruling had it been authored by a man instead of a woman?"

In support of Ömeroğlu, we are publishing her recent cartoon, Freedom of Speech.

World In Focus: Argentina

Since his election in late 2023, far-right libertarian president Javier Milei has taken a no-holds barred approach to unravelling the fabric of Argentina, making drastic cuts and changes wherever he sees fit. Free expression may have been thrown to the wayside

1 Buenos Aires – book censorship

Victoria Villarruel, vice-president of Argentina, wrote a scathing post on X aimed at the governor of Buenos Aires, Axel Kicillof, accusing him of distributing the feminist book Cometierra in classrooms. She labelled the book as "degrading and immoral", posting out-of-context quotes from the book that detailed sexual scenes, and called for it to be banned in schools and public libraries, in the latest attack by Milei's government on sexual education for children. Dolores Reyes, author of Cometierra, received hundreds of death threats following the government's denunciation of her novel, which is a story based on femicide and violence in Argentina. Following this attempted censorship of her work, Reyes told media outlet Infobae: "Silencing is one of the most effective weapons of gender-based violence."

2 Patagonia – the climate crisis

The picturesque mountainous region of Patagonia has suffered from intense wildfires that are currently ravaging the Indigenous areas of the province. Many Mapuche people have been forced to abandon their homes in the heart of the Andes mountains as hillsides are set ablaze. But Milei has denied any possible climate causes for these fires – he has denounced the climate crisis as a "socialist lie" and his sweeping cuts to environmental agencies have decimated Argentina's ability to respond to the wildfires. The National Fire Management System saw a cut of more than 80% in 2024. Instead, authorities carried out raids and arrests on the Mapuche people, accusing them of arson and arresting them, confiscating books and destroying radio equipment in what the community has described as an infringement of their rights. Acts of violence have been common, as the government sees the Indigenous people of Patagonia and other Argentinian regions as obstacles for resource extraction – and with Milei repealing key protections for Indigenous communities, this can be expected to continue.

3 Buenos Aires – court appointments

Milei has made the controversial decision to push through the nomination of two Supreme Court judges by decree, forcing them through while congress was on summer recess. Federal judge Ariel Lijo and lawyer Manuel García-Mansilla had been nominated by Milei in 2024, but they did not gain Senate approval. Milei's camp argue that it is within his constitutional rights to appoint them in this manner as the Supreme Court had two vacancies on its five-person council. However, Human Rights Watch has condemned the move as "one of the most serious attacks against the independence of the Supreme Court in Argentina since the return of democracy". The appointment of Lijo, in particular, proved surprising even to Milei's most ardent supporters: Lijo was a part of the so-called "political elites" that Milei had denounced in his presidential campaign. The judge has been dogged by controversy, with allegations of conspiracy, ethics violations and money laundering levelled against him.

The Index

TECH WATCH

UK wants Apple's most encrypted data

Secret demands to open a backdoor have been revealed, writes **MARK STIMPSON**

IN A TRUMP 2.0 world where Elon Musk acts like an unelected vice-president, you might expect Index on Censorship to be calling out the US government on its tech overreach. Yet in this issue's Tech Watch, it is the UK that is drawing our criticism.

On 7 February, The Washington Post published an exclusive claiming that the UK had ordered Apple to give it a backdoor into its users' most encrypted data. This is information held on iCloud as part of the company's Advanced Data Protection programme where a user's data is end-to-end encrypted and which even Apple cannot access.

The article revealed that the UK government had issued what is known as a technical capability notice under the amended Investigatory Powers Act (IPA), which became law last year.

Under the IPA, it can issue a notice to force technology and communications companies – including social platforms and messaging services – to grant it backdoor access to encrypted data and prevent those companies from disclosing that such a request has been made.

We asked the Home Office about the request and were told: "We do not comment on operational matters, including, for example, confirming or denying the existence of any such notices.

"The Investigatory Powers Act 2016 is designed to protect the public from criminals, child sex abusers and terrorists. With strong independent oversight, the act regulates how intrusive investigatory powers by public authorities are used."

The move has attracted widespread criticism, not only for wanting to break encryption but also because it wants this access for everyone, everywhere.

End-to-end encryption is a vital protection for political dissidents and human rights activists. Index regularly uses encrypted messaging services to communicate with its contributors around the world. A backdoor to that encryption puts them at enormous risk.

Last year, Apple submitted evidence to the UK parliament's Public Bill Committee on the amendments to the IPA, objecting to the proposed reforms.

The company said: "The breadth of these reforms is unprecedented, and the potential impact on the security of technology users across the world cannot be understated."

In an article for Techdirt, writer Mike Masnick wrote: "You can't create a backdoor that only works for 'good guys'. Any vulnerability built into the system becomes a vulnerability for everyone – state actors, cybercriminals and hostile nations alike."

Ron Wyden, a Democrat senator in the USA, posted on Bluesky: "Trump and Apple better tell the UK to go to hell with its demand to access Americans' private, encrypted texts and files. Trump and American tech companies letting

ABOVE: Apple: "We have never built a backdoor"

foreign governments secretly spy on Americans would be an unmitigated privacy and national security disaster."

On 21 February, Apple said it would no longer offer advanced data protection to UK users and issued a statement saying: "As we have said many times before, we have never built a backdoor or master key to any of our products, and we never will."

Andrew Crocker, surveillance litigation director at the Electronic Frontier Foundation, told Index: "Despite the scope of the IPA, I don't think the UK government has, or should have, the power to demand Apple break encryption for users outside its territory.

"Notably, the USA passed a law called the Cloud Act, which creates a framework for data requests from American companies by other countries when that data is held in the USA, but this framework was explicitly 'encryption neutral', meaning that it was not intended to give the UK additional ability to demand backdoors."

Index has now signed a joint letter with Fair Vote UK, Reporters Without Borders, Big Brother Watch and Privacy International urging home secretary Yvette Cooper to answer a number of questions about the request.

In March, Apple said it had appealed against the request with the Investigatory Powers Tribunal. ✖

FEATURES

"In Myanmar, everyone has a list of criminal charges. If they want to arrest you, they will always have a reason to do so"

KEYBOARD WARRIORS | LAURA O'CONNOR | P.40

Rape, reputation and little recourse

Sexual assault victims on India's university campuses are being urged to keep quiet, report **SAMRIDHI KAPOOR** and **HANAN ZAFFAR**

WHEN A 31-YEAR-OLD trainee doctor was found raped and murdered at RG Kar Medical College in the east Indian state of Kolkata last August, outrage swept across the campus. She had fallen asleep in a seminar room after a 36-hour shift and her body was discovered the next day.

Students and other women poured into the streets in their thousands to demand justice, but their voices were quickly stifled. Police detained them, and those who spoke out found themselves under scrutiny.

The incident was not an aberration. For many in the country, this tragedy accentuated an unsettling truth: in India's universities, victims of sexual assault – and those who support them – are often silenced.

Despite laws designed to protect women from harassment, many students and activists say the country's universities have systemic flaws that allow sexual violence to persist.

Across India, students, activists and faculty members describe a culture where voices challenging sexual violence are suppressed to protect the institutions' reputations.

Shabnam Hashmi, a prominent activist based in New Delhi, believes this silencing reflects India's deep-rooted patriarchy, worsened by institutional apathy and the government's preference for symbolic gestures over substantive change.

"Until we challenge the structures that protect perpetrators and shame victims, nothing will change," she said. "Real change begins not only with enforcing laws but with reshaping how we view honour and accountability."

She added that even if victims spoke out, they – not the perpetrators – were held responsible.

In Indian society, victims of sexual harassment often face intense scrutiny and blame while perpetrators are shielded by deeply entrenched patriarchal norms. Instead of holding the harasser accountable, society frequently shifts its focus to the victim, questioning her behaviour, clothing or character. Social honour is often tied to women's bodies, leading survivors to prioritise reputation over justice and discouraging them from speaking out.

Institutional silence

Riya (not her real name), a student at a private university in Haryana, knows firsthand the consequences of speaking up. After a classmate pressured her into sharing intimate photos and then blackmailed her, she wanted to report him. But fear stopped her.

"I was scared [the authorities] would see me as the problem," she told Index. "I didn't think they would help me. My family would have been humiliated and people would just talk."

Her fears had a strong basis. Even though the Prevention of Sexual

> Until we challenge the structures that protect perpetrators and shame victims, nothing will change

CREDIT: David Talukdar/Alamy

ABOVE: Thousands gathered to protest in Kolkata after a 31-year-old trainee doctor was raped and murdered at the city's RG Kar Medical College

Harassment of Women at Workplace (PoSH) Act mandates that all institutions should establish internal complaints committees (ICCs) to handle cases of sexual harassment, many universities either do not have these committees or fail to give them meaningful authority.

"PoSH committees usually only make recommendations," Hashmi said. "They are expected to take action, but the administration often intervenes to protect the institution's image."

This leaves victims with limited avenues for recourse, and for many students the price of speaking out is simply too high.

The problem extends beyond →

The shame is on us, even when we are the ones hurt

→ insufficient resources and into a broader culture of institutional suppression. At Delhi University, external ICC member Vibha Chaturvedi said that many students didn't know how to navigate the complaints process – and when they did, they were often discouraged.

"There is an incredible reluctance to go through the formal process," she said. "Students fear retaliation, ridicule and even academic penalties if they come forward."

Tanisha (not her real name), a student from a prestigious college in Maharashtra, recalls her ordeal with a professor who sexually harassed her.

"I was terrified to report him," she said. "I thought no one would believe me, and the college would protect him. I was very scared. I thought they would think it was somehow my fault, because that is the usual response everywhere."

The concern over protecting the institution's image is so pervasive that students are often actively discouraged from making complaints in the first place.

"From students to faculty to administration, everyone indirectly suggests against raising formal complaints," Tanisha said.

Symbolic policies

The government's approach to women's safety in recent years has been marked by high-profile initiatives, such as the *Beti Bachao, Beti Padhao* (Save the Girl Child, Educate the Girl Child) campaign, which has now been running for a decade. Its aim is to reduce gender discrimination and to educate people about gender bias. Yet critics argue that these campaigns prioritise optics over action. Nearly 80% of its funds have been spent on media campaigns, with limited impact on ground-level support for women's safety.

"These policies are just slogans," said Hashmi. "They are meant to make it look like something's being done [but have no] follow-through."

"We are seeing more censorship, more silencing of dissent and an overall lack of prioritisation for women's safety. It's a culture of complicity, where the perpetrator is shielded and the victim is blamed."

Hashmi believes the government's reluctance to seriously address harassment stems from a larger resistance to challenging patriarchy.

"These are just symbolic gestures by a government that is itself intrinsically conservative and anti-women, and doesn't believe in their freedom or freedom of expression," she said.

India faces severe challenges in safeguarding women against sexual harassment and violence, and despite more than 30,000 cases of reported rape every year, low conviction rates hinder their safety and justice. Slow judicial processes prevent many survivors from pursuing charges, while delayed trials often result in insufficient evidence and witness withdrawal, making convictions rare.

Legislative measures such as the 2013 Criminal Law (Amendment) Act, which introduced harsher penalties for sexual violence, have not translated into consistent enforcement.

The situation has grown worse under prime minister Narendra Modi's administration, many activists argue, as political attention on women's safety has waned.

"We are seeing more censorship, more silencing and an overall dismissal of women's safety as a priority," said Hashmi. "It's a climate of fear and complicity."

The cost of challenging harassment can be high. For Riya, the student from Haryana, simply sharing her story with friends took courage – and she still feels haunted by the experience.

"I want to tell others to speak up, but I understand why they don't," she said. "It is like you are putting yourself on trial. The shame is on us, even when we are the ones hurt."

Mary E John, co-head of the Saksham Task Force, knows all too well the delicate balance of power that exists within academic institutions. Established by the government in 2013 in response to the brutal 2012 Delhi gang rape and murder of a medical student, the task force aims to enhance safety for women on campuses and promote gender sensitivity.

She emphasised the hesitance many students felt when confronted with the daunting task of lodging complaints against their institutions.

"Students often feel they lack independence when they have to complain against the institution's power dynamics," she told Index. This fear of retaliation, she notes, often leads to silence.

The challenges for victims escalate when the alleged harassers hold positions of power, such as professors or administrators. Different power dynamics in academic institutions prevent student survivors from reporting harassment.

"I am terrified my grades would suffer, or people would think I am exaggerating," Tanisha said.

As university campuses continue to grapple with the pervasive issue of sexual harassment, it is clear that a seismic shift in cultural attitudes and institutional responses is long overdue.

The increasing number of heinous cases of sexual harassment on campuses and subsequent protests may have sparked national conversations, but they have rarely translated into tangible action. The cycle only repeats itself. ✖

Samridhi Kapoor is a freelance writer who explores the intersection of gender and social issues. She is based in New Delhi

Hanan Zaffar is a journalist and documentary filmmaker based in South Asia

ABOVE: In 2024, protesters on Rustaveli Avenue were met with riot forces using tear gas and water cannons. Many violent and arbitrary arrests were made against demonstrators across the country

Georgian nightmare

Repression is seeping into more and more aspects of life in Georgia, writes **RUTH GREEN**

"NO TO CENSORSHIP" and "No to repression" read the banners unfurled by protesters night after night as they walk along Rustaveli Avenue in Georgia's capital, Tbilisi.

Protests are nothing new to the city's main thoroughfare. But since Prime Minister Irakli Kobakhidze's abrupt decision to suspend EU accession talks late last year, mass demonstrations have taken on renewed intensity as citizens continue to denounce the Georgian Dream's claims of victory in October 2024's parliamentary election.

The authorities' initial response included brutal dispersal tactics, arbitrary detention and torture by *titushky* – government-affiliated thugs – leaving dozens of protesters hospitalised over the course of several nights of clashes.

As the violence unfolded on the streets, Georgian lawmakers were already drafting sweeping legal amendments with the aim of curbing freedom of expression and peaceful assembly.

The rules passed in December included increasing fines for protesters, restricting the use of fireworks and banning facemasks during protests. The changes also made it easier to dismiss civil servants who were critical of the government and appoint more politically loyal replacements. Hundreds have since been sacked.

Despite these measures, peaceful demonstrations continued largely unabated. On 2 February 2025, the authorities again cracked down on protesters. A new package of repressive legislation was passed, this time imposing an outright ban on spontaneous gatherings and demonstrations in closed spaces and buildings. Detention periods and penalties for protest-related offences increased and criticising public officials became a criminal offence.

This phenomenon of repress, rinse, →

We have not witnessed anything like that since the dissolution of the Soviet Union

→ repeat is all part of "the changing face of terror in Georgia", said Tamar Oniani, human rights programme director and deputy chairperson at the Georgian Young Lawyers' Association (GYLA), one of the country's leading human rights watchdogs.

Oniani said the indiscriminate nature of the recent amendments and the speed with which they've been enacted – often initiated and adopted within the space of a week – underline the regime's concerted efforts to use legal instruments as a repressive tool to intimidate civilians.

"It appears the Georgian Dream government is following the same pattern as in 2024: violent crackdowns on protests followed by repressive legislation, signalling a clear effort to shut down dissent and entrench power indefinitely."

GYLA estimates there have been more than 500 unlawful arrests since the end of November and is monitoring hundreds of cases. Those targeted include political opponents, activists, actors, artists, journalists and minors.

"This diverse circle sends the message that nobody is untouchable, even famous faces," said Oniani. "This is really unprecedented. We have not witnessed anything like that since the dissolution of the Soviet Union."

Despite the authorities' increasingly draconian measures to quell protests, Georgians have continued to take to the streets daily in peaceful defiance against the regime and Russian-style repression.

Muzzled media

Even before Kobakhidze's controversial election win, which was plagued with accusations of vote-rigging, his ruling Georgian Dream party pushed through a highly controversial "foreign agent" law in May 2024. This came after weeks of clashes between police and protesters, who claimed the government would use the legislation to stifle dissent. This was then followed in September by the so-called "family values" bill, which prohibits same-sex marriage, adoptions by same sex couples and gender-affirming treatments.

Under the "foreign agent" law, all NGOs and independent media that receive more than 20% of their funding from foreign donors are required to register as "organisations acting in the interest of a foreign power".

Anna Gvarishvili, a journalist and editor based in Tbilisi, said some independent media outlets have identified loopholes to circumvent the law. Many, however, have been forced to lay off their workforces, drastically reducing the number of outlets with enough resources to keep covering the daily protests.

Those left are facing mounting intimidation and harassment. On 11 January, Mzia Amaglobeli, CEO and founder of Batumelebi, one of Georgia's oldest independent media outlets, was arrested for allegedly slapping a police officer during a rally in Batumi after she put a protest sticker on a wall. A few days later Amaglobeli appeared in court, symbolically holding up a copy of Maria Ressa's How to Stand Up to a Dictator. The judge sentenced her to two months in pre-trial detention. She then went on a hunger strike.

The following day, more than 40 television channels and media outlets went on strike demanding her release.

On 4 March, a judge upheld Amaglobeli's pre-trial detention, rejecting the appeal by her lawyers. Amaglobeli held up a piece of paper with the words "Unjust Court" as the decision was read out. She faces up to seven years in prison.

Gvarishvili believes Amaglobeli's arrest speaks volumes about the pressures facing independent media in the country.

"Batumelebi was the only source for people to get information about what was happening in Batumi," Gvarishvili said. "In my mind, arresting her was a way to demoralise the outlet and make them stop caring about covering the protests."

Having fewer independent media outlets also creates more cracks for disinformation to creep in. Ahead of the election, human rights groups criticised fear-mongering political campaigns by Georgian Dream that drew visual comparisons between war-torn Ukraine and the purported "peace" offered by the Georgian government.

Curtailing speech on campus

As with a similar law enacted in Russia in 2012, it's feared that Georgia's "foreign agent" law could easily be expanded to include other sectors.

This includes education, said Gvarishvili, who also runs the Investigative Media Lab at the University of Georgia.

"At first we thought that as an educational institution we were safe, but it's not like that," she said. "At any moment, the law could be applied to the universities as well."

Meanwhile the "family values" law is already having an impact on university life, said Sophie Shamanidi, a professor in classical philology at Tbilisi State University. As if the sweeping anti-LGBTQ+ aspects of the law weren't bad enough, more pernicious aspects of the legislation, including an amendment to the country's Law on Higher Education, are leading to censorship and the systematic dismantling of vital discourse across the country.

The amendment prohibits any acts – including lectures or seminars – that could be seen to "promote" non-biological gender identity, same-sex relationships or incest.

"It means that an 'objective observer' might determine, for example, that a professor discussing the works of the

CREDIT: Zurab Tsertsvadze / AP

renowned Greek poet Constantine Cavafy – [who was known to be gay] – is 'promoting' gay relationships, or that teaching Sophocles' Oedipus Rex is 'positively portraying' incest," Shamanidi said.

The penalties for violating this amendment escalate quickly, with academics risking fines, suspension or imprisonment.

Although Shamanidi hasn't had to make changes to her lectures or reading lists yet, she said she and colleagues across the humanities are on high alert to ensure they don't put a foot wrong.

"The government wants to silence professors who are speaking loudly and who don't like them," she said. "The law represents a tool for Georgian Dream to silence critical thinkers and suppress free expression."

Shamanidi knows this feeling better than most. As an election observer, on 26 October she witnessed two women at a polling station trying to vote more than once, claiming the ink on their fingers was shellac nail polish.

"I saw what they were doing, it was unbelievable," she said. When Shamanidi tried to raise the alarm, she says the women called her a "provocateur". The police were called and the matter was quickly hushed up.

Shamanidi has also seen the lengths to which the government has gone to in order to shut down free speech closer to home. Her husband, Lasha Bugadze, a high-profile Georgian novelist and playwright, speaks regularly on television about the former prime minister and now honorary chairman of Georgian Dream Bidzina Ivanishvili and the government. One day Bugadze's photo appeared on walls all over their neighbourhood with graffiti labelling

ABOVE: Workers wave the Georgian flag during a nationwide strike in Tbilisi in January 2025, carried out in protest at the Georgian Dream government

him an "enemy of the nation" and a "foreign agent". The public response to the attack on her husband was one of peaceful resistance. Overnight, the photos and slogans were replaced with paintings of Georgian, EU and Ukrainian flags and positive messages.

"They did it all at night," Shamanidi said. "We didn't know even who did it. We just saw one day that everything had been cleaned up."

Oniani, from GYLA, said Georgians have largely felt encouraged by the international outrage over the government's repressive tactics throughout the protests. But she believes there should be greater acknowledgement that the country is sliding into Kremlin-style authoritarianism – before it's too late.

"Everybody should understand at an international level that this situation is not solely about certain bills or isolated human rights violations," Oniani said. "They're turning the country into an authoritarian regime. That's not the will of the Georgian people."

In the evenings, as Georgians continue to protest, the theatres remain closed and the restaurants lining Rustaveli Avenue lie empty. This is the "new normal," Gvarishvili said, and Georgians are determined to keep going as long as it takes.

"The history of protests has demonstrated that non-violent, consistent protests in the streets have the ability to collapse a regime," she said. "So that's what we're doing. It's risky. It could end up like Belarus, but I honestly believe that this is the only way to win." ✖

The law represents a tool for Georgian Dream to silence critical thinkers and suppress free expression

Ruth Green is a journalist who writes about law, business and human rights

Botswana's new era

CLEMENCE MANYUKWE explores whether Duma Boko, the country's newly elected president, could usher in positive change

WHEN THE BUSHMEN were evicted from their ancestral lands in Botswana's Central Kalahari Game Reserve in the 1990s, they turned to UK-based human rights group Survival International for help.

The Bushmen – also known as the San and the Basarwa – are Botswana's Indigenous hunters and gatherers. Survival International, which campaigns for the rights of Indigenous and tribal people, was willing to fund a legal challenge to fight the group's eviction, but there was one problem – the government was torturing the Bushmen and harassing those speaking on their behalf.

There were no takers for the Bushmen's cause as people were afraid. However, a young human rights lawyer named Duma Gideon Boko stepped forward.

He sued the government on behalf of the tribe in a legal case that defined his career.

"The fact that Duma and his legal firm took on the Bushmen court case against a powerful government when other lawyers declined to work on it demonstrates his independence of mind and commitment to defending Indigenous rights," Paula Zamorano Osorio, Survival International's media and communications officer, told Index.

Survival International became involved in the court case at the request of the Bushmen and the group funded the work of the legal team, which consisted of Boko and UK barrister Gordon Bennett. At one point, Botswana's government denied Bennett a visa, stopping him from travelling to Botswana and leaving Boko to fight the case alone.

But in a landmark decision on 13 December 2006, the Botswana High Court ruled that the government's evictions were "unlawful and unconstitutional", so the Bushmen had the right to return to their lands in the game reserve.

No one knew then that the young lawyer who had become a brave voice for justice would one day be elected Botswana's president.

Born in 1969 in the small town of Mahalapye, Boko studied law at the University of Botswana, then went on to obtain a Master's degree from Harvard Law School. He also studied for a diploma in human rights and humanitarian law from Lund University in Sweden.

He went on to establish a prestigious career and held many leadership positions that showed he was destined for greater things.

He became the country's new leader on 1 November last year, with his seismic election victory bringing the 58-year rule of the Botswana Democratic Party (BDP) to an abrupt end. Boko leads the Umbrella for Democratic Change (UDC), a coalition of centre-left and left-wing political parties.

ABOVE: Boko speaks during the African Economic Conference in Gaborone, Botswana in November 2024

This is not his first foray into politics. Since 2010 he has been president of the Botswana National Front, a social democratic party and the main opposition until the 2024 election. He served as the country's leader of the opposition from 2014 to 2019, and led the creation of the UDC.

Boko is also a former chairperson of the Law Society of Botswana and the Botswana Network of Ethics, Law and HIV/Aids, and a former president of the University of Botswana Student Representative Council.

One month after being elected, Boko showed that he had not forgotten about the plight of the Bushmen by allowing them to bury Pitseng Gaoberekwe – a member of the tribe who died in December 2021 – on their ancestral land

ABOVE: Duma Boko waves to crowds at his inauguration ceremony in Gaborone, Botswana on 8 November 2024

in the Central Kalahari Reserve. The courts had previously barred the family from burying him there due to the forced displacement of the tribal group, and his body had been kept in a mortuary for more than two years.

Survival International's Osorio said many sectors of Botswana's society were hostile to the Bushmen who, as hunter gatherers, were regarded as inferior by the majority cattle-owners. Boko has been influential in reshaping public opinion so that they have started to be regarded as individuals with equal rights.

She added that Boko's work on the case had created a lasting legacy for Bushmen and other minority groups in Botswana who have suffered decades of racism and discrimination from consecutive governments.

Another cause he has championed has been LGBTQ+ rights. Caine Youngman, a human rights activist who led the fight against the country's ban on consensual same-sex relationships, told Index that Boko volunteered to represent him long before he became president. The pair have collaborated on human rights issues for the past 15 years.

"He has always had an interest in human rights, particularly for the LGBTQI community," said Youngman. "Initially we had our first decriminalisation case, which was in my name – Caine Youngman v the State. We were seeking to do away with the penal code provisions that criminalised same-sex sexual behaviour."

In a strategic move, the pair ended up withdrawing the case to deal with an "easier victory" first – a court challenge asking the government to register

> The fact that Duma took on the Bushmen court case against a powerful government demonstrates his independence of mind

CREDIT: (main) Associated Press / Alamy; (inset) Tshekiso Tebalo / Xinhua / Alamy

the Lesbians, Gays and Bisexuals of Botswana group, which they won in 2014 with a different lawyer.

"After the victory of registering the organisation, we used that to relaunch the decriminalisation case," he added. They won the case in 2019 and the ruling was upheld in 2021 after a government appeal against it was dismissed.

On top of his work representing marginalised communities, Boko is also a free-speech crusader, according to Youngman. His law firm has offered free legal services to university students who speak truth to power.

"The University of Botswana has always had a strong student representative council, which most of the time has gone at loggerheads against the university administration or the Ministry of Health," said Youngman.

He added that by offering free legal aid, Boko has helped to protect freedom of expression for students and has given them a platform to express themselves and challenge the powers that be.

Alice Mogwe, the president of the International Federation for Human Rights and director of the Botswana Centre for Human Rights, highlighted

ABOVE: Duma Boko was sworn in as Botswana's president on 1 November 2024, bringing the 58-year rule of the Botswana Democratic Party (BDP) to an abrupt end

In our human-rights-led government, no citizen will be undermined

Boko's credentials as an abolitionist who has taken on a number of death penalty cases over the years.

One client, Brandon Sampson, was on death row while awaiting the outcome of a Court of Appeal trial. The hearing in 2011 led to his death penalty being removed, and a 20-year jail term being imposed instead. He completed community service and was released in 2013, and is now "reportedly a productive member of society", said Mogwe.

"Over the years, President Boko has expressed his opposition to the death penalty, including before the courts during his defence of those charged with a capital offence," Mogwe told Index over email. "We look forward to serious consideration of the imposition of a moratorium on the death penalty, which will be in keeping with the human rights-based approach to governance espoused by the new government.

"We also look forward to a serious reflection of how to consciously apply contextualised human rights values in governance and [to] the economy."

But how much of a "human rights-based approach" will Boko really take in his governing?

He pledged to do this during his election campaign, and his party's manifesto backs up this ideology. It promises to usher in a new democratic constitution and herald far-reaching societal changes. Issues that Boko has spoken out on include increasing migrant rights – such as helping undocumented Zimbabweans become legal by granting them temporary work and residence permits – supporting young people, and raising basic pay.

The UDC manifesto reads: "The current constitution is built upon patriarchal, ethnic, cultural and age inequalities of the old society and has, over the 60 years of the BDP rule, simply reproduced these inequalities.

"Together with the people of Botswana, we will act to establish a body and mechanism within the confines of the law to set in motion a comprehensive review and public engagement (people-driven, participatory, inclusive and transparent) for a new constitution crafted to offer our nation an inclusive government system."

It says that the new constitution will have checks and balances to fight corruption and curb abuses of power; provide impeachment articles for the head of state and a recall system for elected representatives; and provide for the direct election of the president and abolish the "automatic succession clause". The succession clause means that if a president dies, resigns or ceases to hold office (outside of an election), the vice-president becomes president.

The manifesto also promises to "drastically reduce" the powers of the president by giving parliament or special organisations the responsibility of appointing people to senior government positions. It also pledges to reform the electoral system and establish an Independent Electoral Commission.

Only time will tell if Boko will stay the course on his human rights promises. But on 10 December last year – Human Rights Day – he said that his government was committed to placing human rights at the core of its policies, and he promised that injustices, such as those committed against the Basarwa people, would not be repeated: "In our human-rights-led government, no citizen will be undermined." ✖

Clemence Manyukwe is a Zimbabwean human rights journalist covering African affairs

Venezuela's prison problem

From inhumane conditions to unjust detentions, **CATHERINE ELLIS** explores the plight of political prisoners in the Latin American country

ABOVE: Protesters call for democracy, standing against Nicolás Maduro and in support of Edmundo González Urrutia in Madrid in January

WHEN LAWYER PERKINS Rocha was seized by forces while leaving a pharmacy in Caracas on 27 August 2024, his family found out he had been taken only when they saw a post on social media platform X.

A frantic investigation began to find out where Rocha, the legal co-ordinator for Venezuela's election campaign for the political opposition, was being held – and to speak to those who had seen what had happened.

"Witnesses told us that hooded men approached him and a strong struggle began. They hit him and dragged him to one of the unmarked vehicles they were in, and took him away," his son Santiago told Index.

The family haven't seen or heard from him since.

The highest number of political prisoners in Latin America

Rocha's case is far from an isolated one. According to human rights organisation Foro Penal, Venezuela had 1,196 political prisoners as of 3 February 2025.

The country has the most political prisoners in Latin America – followed by Cuba with 1,150 – and has a history of using repression and arbitrary detentions as a means of silencing and punishing those with anti-government views.

This pattern has intensified following the July 2024 presidential election, which incumbent Nicolás Maduro insisted he won despite evidence from voting tally receipts showing opposition candidate Edmundo González Urrutia won by a landslide with 67% of the vote.

LEFT: Maduro insists he won the 2024 presidential election in Venezuela, despite voting tallies showing the opposition candidate González Urrutia won by a landslide. Here, Maduro addresses his supporters in Caracas in February

→ Protests demanding that the state acknowledge the opposition's legitimate win followed, and with them a swathe of arrests and detentions during random street searches by police looking for content on people's phones that criticised the government. Others were detained during Operation Knock Knock, where security forces arrived at people's houses (often late at night) to arrest them and take them to prison.

Arbitrary detentions designed to force dissenters to stay silent started well before last year's election. But according to human rights group The Venezuelan Education-Action Programme on Human Rights (Provea), the sheer number of arrests in a short space of time during the 2024 crackdown was on a different level from previous years. Between 29 July and 13 August, roughly 2,400 people were arrested, which is an average of 150 arrests a day.

It is not only the scale of detentions that highlights the intensified repression but also the charges against those being held. According to Marino Alvarado, legal action co-ordinator at Provea, all the prisoners were initially charged with terrorism, including children and teenagers. Maduro referred to those detained as "terrorists" in a televised address.

"In some cases, in addition to the crime of terrorism, [they were charged with] treason, criminal association and other crimes, but all were tried by anti-terrorism courts," Alvarado told Index.

Legal representation is also unsatisfactory, with public lawyers being "imposed" on political prisoners rather than them having the option to choose a "trusted, private lawyer".

"In addition to having a lot of work, public lawyers receive direct orders from the state, and detained people are left without the right to a defence," said Alvarado.

Dire conditions within prisons

Conditions within prisons are notoriously grim. Some do not permit visits from families, but others allow them every 15 days – although sometimes these are cancelled by the authorities. When people do see their loved ones, it is often a heart-wrenching experience.

"I noticed he was shaky and nervous and I asked him what was wrong," said Maritza, whose name has been changed for her own safety and for that of her son, who was detained a few days after the July 2024 protests. She described him as a young man who was normally calm and confident.

"Eventually he said to me, 'Mum, when I get out of here I'm going to tell you everything I've been through, but while I'm here I'm going to keep quiet and endure what I'm living [through] because I don't want to anger [the authorities].'"

A report from the Committee for the Freedom of Political Prisoners (CLIPPVE) highlighted that food rations inside the prisons were often tiny and insufficient, sometimes contained insects and were rotten or not sufficiently cooked. The information is based on testimonies from families of those in jail, as well as ex-prisoners. Many of the prisoners have lost weight and have experienced stomach illnesses.

One woman whose son has been held in Tocuyito Prison said she couldn't even recognise him when she saw him. "He was so thin and malnourished that I had him in front of me and I wouldn't know it was him," she said.

In November and December, three political prisoners died. One of them, Jesús Manuel Martínez Medina, was detained on 29 July and allegedly

> We don't know if my dad has seen the sun in days, weeks or months, if he has eaten well or if they have tortured him

mistreated and denied the necessary medical care to treat his Type II diabetes, according to CLIPPVE. The NGO says the 36-year-old's health deteriorated rapidly due to lack of treatment. Although he was transferred to hospital, he died on 14 November during an operation to amputate his legs.

Medical attention is severely lacking in the prisons. Santiago Rocha said he was constantly worried about the health of his father, who suffers from hydrocephalus – a build-up of fluid in the brain. He has a fitted valve connected from his brain to his stomach to drain the fluid.

"We always have this fear that no one is watching him, no one is checking on him. Any blow or movement that is abrupt could alter the functioning of that valve and the hose," the 30-year-old said.

He eventually discovered his father had been taken to el Helicoide, a notorious jail known for holding political prisoners and for its use of torture. "We don't know if my dad has seen the sun in days, weeks or months, if he has eaten well or if they have tortured him," he added.

Erosion of a democratic state

Some of those taken have been tortured. One of those is Jesús Armas, an engineer, human rights activist and member of the opposition campaign team, who was taken by hooded individuals on 10 December 2024 while leaving a restaurant in Caracas and whose whereabouts were not known for days.

"His girlfriend managed to see him for 15 minutes before he was transferred to el Helicoide prison. He told her he had been held in a clandestine house, suffocated with a bag and left tied to a chair for several days," said Genesis Davila, a lawyer and founder of Defiende Venezuela, an organisation that presents human rights violations in Venezuela to international legal institutions.

As is the case with many political prisoners, public prosecutors, judges and defence lawyers denied knowing about Armas's detention for days.

Venezuelans have no recourse if they suffer abuse at the hands of the government

"But while they said this, Jesús had already been presented before a court, there was already a prosecutor who knew the case and there was also a public defender who had been assigned to [his]' case," Davila said.

Repression has intensified under the socialist regime. When Hugo Chávez first took office in 1999, he did so on a wave of popular support and spent huge amounts on social programmes such as adult literacy projects and free community healthcare for impoverished communities, largely funded by the country's oil wealth.

But alongside this he started to concentrate power, taking control of the Supreme Court and undermining the ability of journalists, human rights defenders and other Venezuelans to exercise fundamental rights, according to a Human Rights Watch report that reflected on his legacy.

Maduro took over the presidency when Hugo Chávez died of cancer in 2013. A drop in oil prices, mismanagement of resources and corruption led to a dire economic and humanitarian crisis (exacerbated by US sanctions, according to many analysts). Brutal state crackdowns on anti-government protests in 2014, 2017 and 2019 led to deaths and mass detentions.

For Phil Gunson, a senior analyst at the think-tank International Crisis Group, repression has worsened significantly in Venezuela since 1999. The less popular the government became, the more it used repression to stay in power, which became even clearer in its use of heavy-handed tactics in the 2024 protests.

"The government is entirely dependent on the army and the police," said Gunson. "That doesn't just mean harassing and detaining dissidents but treating them so badly that no one dares to protest."

The analyst says impunity is another reason for rising repression.

"Venezuelans have no recourse if they suffer abuse at the hands of the government, and members of the security forces can be fairly certain there will be no consequences if they commit human rights abuses."

For those with families in prison, their daily nightmare is unbearable – yet they say giving up hope for their loved ones' release and a free Venezuela is not an option.

"I try to keep him in mind as I go about my day-to-day life, asking myself what he would want me to do at this moment," Santiago Rocha said, describing his dad as a loving father and a man with strong ideals.

"I keep him like this so I don't feel far away from him and remember that all the work he – and the people who have worked with him – have done will not be in vain." ✖

ABOVE: (left) Political prisoner Perkins Rocha is currently suffering health issues in prison; (right) Rocha with his son Santiago, who is holding out hope for his father's release

Catherine Ellis is a British journalist who reports from Colombia and Venezuela

ABOVE: The police impound a vehicle before a protest against Salman Rushdie in New Delhi, India in 2012

Forbidden words

The ban on Salman Rushdie's The Satanic Verses has been lifted in India after nearly four decades, but its absence from bookshelves continues, writes **SALIL TRIPATHI**

WRITERS FROM AROUND the world head for India each winter, criss-crossing the vast country to participate in dozens of literature festivals. Each festival has a bookshop, where writers are invited to sign their books. This winter I took part in six festivals and visited more than a dozen stores across different cities – but I saw Salman Rushdie's The Satanic Verses in only one.

It made a quiet appearance at Bahrisons Booksellers in Delhi, but I didn't see it displayed anywhere else. It has since been reported that it is on sale in a few stores, although a search on Amazon's Indian website in early February did not show the novel at all.

This is most peculiar, but not more so than the circumstances surrounding the novel's reappearance. India banned Rushdie's book in 1988 (the year it was published). It was the first country to do so but last year it overturned its decision, meaning the book could be imported for the first time in 36 years.

This was not a government attempt to suddenly uphold free speech but was due to a strange legal technicality that bordered on hilarious. In 2017, a West Bengal resident called Sandipan Khan filed a Right to Information request for access to the official notification banning the book's import, as he wanted to read the novel. When the government could not find the notification, he took the matter to the Delhi High Court in 2019, arguing that it restricted his right to read.

After five years of the government searching to no avail, the court had no option but to presume it did not exist, so the import ban was lifted in November. If the order did not exist in physical or electronic form, how could the court surmise that it ever existed?

This was Kafkaesque bureaucracy at its finest and could itself be turned into a comic novel. But the ban was no laughing matter.

In October 1988, within days of India Today publishing excerpts from The Satanic Verses, protests erupted in India, and Muslim leaders and intellectuals campaigned to Rajiv Gandhi's government to ban the book. Many had not read it but had heard, or been told, that it was offensive – some literature experts I interviewed at the time told me that there was no need for them to read it as they had already made up their minds. "A novel should be about things that ennoble the mind, not about things that hurt readers' feelings," one professor of English literature told me.

In any case, Rushdie's Indian publisher, Penguin Random House India, was advised by its editorial advisers not to publish it there. The only way the book could legitimately get to the country was by being imported, and the customs department issued a notification prohibiting that.

Rushdie's myriad fans in India were stunned, but the government cited the need to maintain law and order amid fears of public unrest. Indeed, after Iran's Ayatollah Khomeini issued a fatwa on Rushdie on Valentine's Day 1989, mass demonstrations took place across India.

As a young reporter in Rushdie's hometown Mumbai (then known as Bombay), I saw police shoot at a procession of young Muslim men marching towards the British Council Library that had turned violent, and a dozen demonstrators died. Those who justified the ban felt vindicated. In the years since, Rushdie's Japanese translator Hitoshi Igarashi was fatally stabbed in 1991; his Norwegian publisher William Nygaard was shot in 1993; and Rushdie himself was stabbed multiple times and nearly died (he lost an eye) in an attack in the USA in 2022. Not only did he survive but he wrote a moving and courageous memoir, Knife, published in 2024.

The recent Delhi court order has removed the obstacle facing retailers wanting to import the book. Rushdie is a popular author in India, and his other novels are easily available. One might think Penguin or another publisher would want to secure rights to publish it in India. But this does not seem to have happened.

It is not known how the government would react if any publisher were to publish The Satanic Verses in India. Narendra Modi's government is fiercely Hindu nationalist and has been in power since 2014, winning a majority in two elections and emerging as the single-largest party in the 2024 elections. It now leads a coalition.

Over the past decade, attacks on Muslims have increased and discrimination has become more brazen. Muslims are more likely than other groups to get arrested for alleged anti-national activities. Government bulldozers raze their homes for petty reasons (or for no reason), it is harder for them to rent or buy property, and Muslim-owned businesses are discriminated against – with some states requiring shop and restaurant owners to display their names publicly for customers. A new citizenship law that would be used to denationalise Indian Muslims who cannot show documentation of their citizenship has also rung alarm bells.

Some have argued that if a book as emotive as The Satanic Verses gets published in India or is imported and distributed by Indian retailers, it could become the spark that provokes conflagration.

But over the years, Indian society has come to place the rights of the offended on a higher plane than the rights of those who express their views. Security is considered more important than liberty.

The absence of The Satanic Verses from Indian bookshelves has been

ABOVE: Protesters in Kashmir burn an effigy of British author Salman Rushdie in June 2007, in outrage at his British knighthood

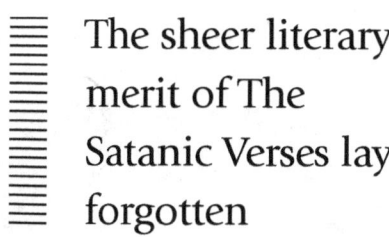

The sheer literary merit of The Satanic Verses lay forgotten

a stain on the country's professed commitment to freedom of expression. Rushdie placed writing from India on the global map with his 1981 novel Midnight's Children. His profound understanding of his homeland, deep love for its syncretic culture, knowledge of Indian history and myths, and vivid imagination encouraged a generation of Indians to own the English language and express themselves with confidence.

True, India has a long tradition of writing in English and a rich range of voices in Indian languages, but Rushdie's brilliance opened the door for Indians aspiring to make their mark internationally. It was the empire striking back. The absence of his major novel emboldened other people claiming offence to get works of art, books or films banned in India.

And amid the hullabaloo, the sheer literary merit of The Satanic Verses lay forgotten. It is perhaps the most important novel of the last century, reflecting on the meaning and impact of migration, where belief begins and reason ends, and the power of myth over reality. It captures the disturbances brought on by modernity, destabilising the moral certainties of a universe set in stone.

It shows our hybrid identities in the post-colonial world. And its wider access could give readers in India an opportunity to see the novel for what it is rather than how it is described: not necessarily an attack on a faith but a reflection on the human condition. ✖

Salil Tripathi is a contributing editor for Index on Censorship

The art of resistance

Tunisia's creative scene is pushing back against President Kais Saied's control. **ALESSANDRA BAJEC** explores three artistic endeavours that are breaking boundaries, and which were all spotlighted at the Nawaat Festival

YASSINE ALOUINI, A young filmmaker, was visiting his hometown Kairouan in the centre of Tunisia, when he had the idea for his short film Décret 25.07. The inspiration came to him after he saw roughly 50 Black people fleeing the city on foot. It was late February 2023, three days before President Kais Saied made a speech claiming that irregular migration from sub-Saharan Africa was aimed at creating a "purely African country that has no affiliation to the Arab and Islamic nations". The hateful speech unleashed a wave of violence against Black Africans.

Shocked by what he witnessed, Alouini remembers: "I imagined a decree creating a new job, that of 'bounty hunters', who would be financially compensated for assisting police in chasing irregular migrants."

Within two hours, he had started writing the script for Décret 25.07. Its title clearly alludes to President Saied's 25 July 2021 coup, which marked the shift to a highly authoritarian, presidential regime.

ABOVE: Heat Hit is the first graffiti archive in Tunisia, a scene that emerged after the Tunisian revolution

Set in 2025, in the midst of a worsening displacement crisis, the story set in Tunisia recounts the last night of an undocumented couple from the Ivory Coast en route to Europe. The president has recently issued a decree inviting citizens to collaborate with law enforcement in targeting migrants, and a group of bounty hunters decide to disrupt the young couple's plans.

"Those who choose to leave their country do so because they've lost hope and are searching for a better life elsewhere," Alouini said, rejecting the racist treatment Tunisians face in Europe, similar to the discrimination Sub-Saharan Africans experience in his homeland.

Black migrants have become a scapegoat for Tunisia's intractable economic and social crisis. The president's anti-migrant rhetoric and the surge in violent racism across the country have pushed more African nationals to flee and the North African state has emerged as a key transit point for sub-Saharan migrants and asylum seekers.

Alouini claimed he has "no limits" in tackling certain topics, regardless of whether they are sensitive, though he admitted that others in the artistic community cannot express themselves freely, fearing state censorship and jail time. He recalled the day when the film's editor asked to have his name left off the credits, as they were piecing together scenes from Décret 25.07.

"We know we're under some kind of dictatorship. I see how my colleagues are affected. Many no longer want to take risks," Alouini said.

In his experience, most independent artists stay true to their views and bring them to life despite the lack of funding, limited opportunities and the challenges of operating under the growing authoritarian rule of President Saied. Alouini is confident that nothing will stop him from speaking his mind. He believes there are acts of resistance within Tunisia's art space where creatives continue to work independently, each striving to do their best, and engaging in alternative forms of expression.

"No matter what, there will always be a vocal minority. That's all we have left," he said. "Since the 2011 revolution we can't be silenced."

Taking to the streets

Ameni Ghimagi is the co-producer of Heat Hit, the first graffiti archive in Tunisia. She works with Ilyes Louati, a young cultural entrepreneur. During her teens, Ghimagi was tagging walls, which her parents saw as an act of vandalism.

"The walls I grew up around as a teenager really stuck with me. I couldn't paint graffiti but I always found it impressive," she said.

Ghimagi told Index that Tunisia's rich, dynamic street art scene emerged after the uprising that led to the fall of long-time dictator Zine al-Abidine Ben Ali in 2011, highlighting how walls covered in writings and drawings serve as a canvas for the country's history.

She noted that traces of countless graffiti pieces are now hard to find, whether they were worn out by the weather, erased or covered up.

"80% of the murals that we catalogued no longer exist," she said. "Heat Hit is more than just a beautiful compilation of artworks, it's a project that pays tribute to the artists who are behind those walls so they're not forgotten."

She suggested that graffitists are often excluded from official discourse, dismissed and seen by the state as drifters.

Looking back at the outburst of artistic production during and after the Tunisian revolution, Ghimagi highlighted how urban art served as a means to make a statement, and reclaim the public space that had long been denied. Today, she hopes to help preserve this art and make it last in a country where creative talent abounds, but public venues for alternative forms of art remain scarce.

ABOVE: No Paradise Beneath Their Feet puts the taboo of non-motherhood on the Tunisian stage

Reflecting on Tunisia's shrinking civic space, where few dare to speak openly, Ghimagi urged artists to remain authentic and resist censorship.

"We must not forget [what] we've experienced before. We need to keep speaking up," she insisted. "If we stay quiet, we will only allow anyone to restrict or deny us our freedoms."

Once considered a beacon of hope for democracy in the Arab region, Tunisia has seen significant democratic backsliding since Saied assumed full control in 2021. The autocratic →

> We know we're under some kind of dictatorship. I see how my colleagues are affected; many no longer want to take risks

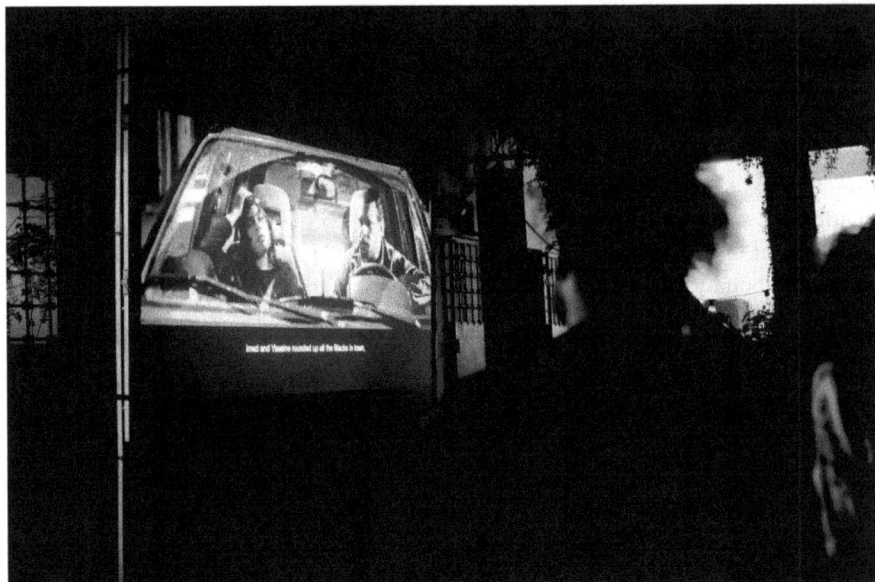

RIGHT: A screening of Décret 25.07, a film inspired by the violent fallout of President Kais Saied's hateful rhetoric towards Black Africans

→ president has tightened his grip on Tunisia's institutions and enacted his own decree laws that severely limit freedom of expression. In the last two years, he has used the draconian Decree Law 54, which criminalises the spread of "false information".

Dissenting voices are being repressed, with journalists, lawyers, political opponents, artists, dissidents and human rights defenders imprisoned.

Putting taboos on stage

No Paradise Beneath Their Feet, a play by actor and theatre director Mouna Ben Haj Zekri and Egyptian researcher and performer Mai Choucri deals with the issue of non-motherhood, a subject few Tunisian women feel bold enough to discuss.

When her co-producer proposed the idea for the show, Ben Haj Zekri immediately connected with the topic, as a childless woman herself with "no paradise beneath her feet".

Based on the testimonies of six women, the theatrical reading explores the experiences and emotions of both those who have chosen not to become mothers and those who have not been able to have children.

Since the early stages of the play's pre-production, the two artists realised that non-motherhood is an unspoken, painful topic. For all the women they met, it was the first time they had talked about it.

No Paradise Beneath Their Feet takes a deep look into the realities of those who do not conform to motherhood and challenge the societal norm of childbearing.

"I discovered what it's like for women undergoing medically assisted

procreation. They cling to a fragile hope, facing high costs, no psychological assistance, and often lacking family support," Ben Haj Zekri said.

She explored some difficult questions and debates within the theatrical piece: the rejection of egg freezing as part of a capitalist plan to delay motherhood; the difference between single mothers – who are in an unchosen, precarious situation – and solo mothers, who are in a privileged position of choice; the financial challenge of a woman raising a child on her own; the right of all women, regardless of their gender expression, to become mothers.

Ben Haj Zekri said that despite the odds, Tunisians continue to push boundaries in creative circles like cinema and theatre.

"Bans or restrictions won't stop us," she vowed. "What matters to me is that drama stays real, and as artists we stay as close as possible to our real-life experiences." ✖

Alessandra Bajec is an independent journalist who specialises in the Middle East and North Africa region

Walls covered in writings and drawings serve as a canvas for the country's history

ABOVE: A school and its library in the Donetsk region of Ukraine destroyed by rocket and artillery fire

A tragic renaissance

EMILY COUCH explores how, amid devastation, Ukrainians are embracing their literary culture more than ever before

FOR THOSE OF us lucky enough to live in a country not experiencing the ravages of war, the old adage about the pen being mightier than the sword may sound trite. But in Ukraine, while literature cannot deflect Russian bullets, it fights the chilling purpose behind them.

In 2021, in an essay titled On the Historical Unity of Russians and Ukrainians, Russian president Vladimir Putin claimed that the two countries shared a "common literary and cultural heritage", belying Russia's centuries-long attempts to suppress Ukraine's language and literature. While this policy began in the 17th century, it gained intensity in the twilight years of the Russian Empire.

The Soviet Union under Joseph Stalin took this policy to its extreme, executing hundreds of Ukrainian intellectuals, including writers.

Russia's brutal full-scale invasion of Ukraine appears to be a continuation of this policy, destroying hundreds of culturally significant buildings – including libraries – and killing writers on the frontline and during attacks on civilian targets. Yet, by targeting their culture, Russia has spurred Ukrainians to embrace it more than ever before, giving rise to a literary renaissance amid the horrors of war.

Index interviewed three Ukrainians representing organisations and initiatives at the forefront of this phenomenon.

Chytomo

Iryna Baturevych co-founded Chytomo – a media outlet dedicated to Ukrainian literature – in 2009. According to the Ukrainian Publishers and Booksellers Association (UPBA), until 2017, books imported from Russia accounted →

for roughly 75% of the Ukrainian publishing market. These books often perpetuated Russian propaganda, said Baturevych – including "narratives suggesting Ukraine was a 'fake state'… many of the negative characters in these stories were Ukrainian, portrayed as 'provincials', 'simple minded', 'losers' or 'betrayers'". The Ukrainian government did little to stop this or support Ukrainian literature, she said. Chytomo was born of the desire to buck the trend.

Although Russia began its war on Ukraine in 2014, it was the full-scale invasion of 2022 that spurred a radical transformation in Ukraine's literary landscape. In June 2022, its parliament voted to ban the printing of books by Russian citizens (unless they renounced their Russian passports and took Ukrainian citizenship), and the import of books printed in Russia.

These laws have elicited debate over the ethics of restricting book imports during times of war; the issue is particularly complex in this context, given Russia's long history of suppressing Ukrainian culture. Baturevych argues that the laws have created space in the market for Ukrainian books and translations to be published and flourish, whereas Russian literature had dominated before. Testament to this is that the number of bookshops in Ukraine has more than doubled, from 222 in 2021 to 500 today, according to Baturevych, and publishers have "finally turned towards young [Ukrainian] talents".

Ukrainians demonstrate their commitment to their country's literature in the most extreme circumstances. Baturevych is chair of the jury for the Chytomo Award, which acknowledges outstanding achievements in Ukrainian book publishing. She highlights the example of Anton Martynov, a publisher who was drafted into the military.

"From his position in the woods in eastern Ukraine, he searches for an internet connection to … ensure the publishing house keeps running. We truly understand the price of literature these days," she said.

Nedopysani

And all too often, that price is the ultimate one. Yevhen Lyr co-founded Nedopysani to commemorate Ukrainian writers killed by Russian forces. "It started as a way of dealing with trauma," explained Lyr, a writer currently serving in the Ukrainian armed forces. The memorial project started as a list of names in a private chat with a fellow poet serving on the frontline, before growing into a public initiative by 2023.

"When I volunteered for the Ukrainian armed forces, it became somewhat of a ritual," he said. "I searched social media and news an hour or two before sleep, and every time new names [of people killed] emerged. As we speak, there are 223 people of literature killed by the Russians on our list."

The aim of Nedopysani is to "create an environment of assurance", where "no writer, translator or publisher will be forgotten".

Like Baturevych, Lyr speaks of how Ukraine's literary culture has blossomed in this most difficult of times.

"Both in 2014 and 2022, the reader's demand for Ukrainian literature rocketed sky-high, and that created a window for plenty of new names and even sub-genres," he said. "Books I could only dream of reading in 2018 are now resting on my bookshelves."

He noted in particular the reprinting of Ukrainian classics, such as Misto by Valerian Pidmohylny, originally published in 1928. "Before that, a lot of readers viewed Ukrainian classics as somewhat boring fiction from school programmes. And here we are, a nearly 100-year-old book tops the book charts in 2023."

Institute for Documentation and Exchange

One writer who symbolises Russia's war on Ukrainian culture and the power of memory is Victoria Amelina. In the summer of 2023, she was touring the country with Colombian writers whom she had invited to document Russian war crimes and build international

LEFT: The building of the Huliaipole District Museum of Local Lore in the city of Polohy in Ukraine was destroyed by Russian shelling on 24 August 2024

RIGHT: A librarian stands in the library of a destroyed village club building in Rudnytske near Kyiv in 2022

support for Ukraine. On 27 June, Amelina was dining in a restaurant in Kramatorsk with one of the group when a Russian missile struck. Four days later, she died from her injuries, aged 37.

Sasha Dovzhyk is the director of INDEX (Institute for Documentation and Exchange), a Lviv-based cultural institution documenting Russia's war and facilitating exchanges between Ukrainian intellectuals and their international peers. In November 2024, it launched the Victoria Amelina Fellowship to honour the writer's memory. "It is a way for us to continue the work that Victoria was so good at – building these bridges of understanding, of compassion, of solidarity, of action," said Dovzhyk.

The fellowship will bring one Ukrainian writer and another from abroad together in Lviv to create a joint project on their experiences in the country.

Dovzhyk highlights how Ukrainian literature has flourished in the face of Russian attempts to destroy it, with book clubs emerging across the country. "Our literature has captured the history of Ukrainian colonisation by neighbouring empires, and it contains some of the strategies of resistance," she said. "So those of us who had next-to-zero interest in Ukrainian writing have turned to the classics."

But resistance is not without cost. Ukrainian literature may be thriving against all odds, but it is indelibly marked by the trauma of war. Dovzhyk notes the development of "documentary poetry", which aims to present people's traumatic experiences of "fighting for survival" in a condensed format. She highlights the example of Kateryna Mikhalytsina, who "writes about the trees as witnesses of Russia's war crimes. The trees that stand burned and naked and leafless in the aftermath of a missile strike on her city".

Ukrainian literature abroad

Is Ukraine's wartime literary renaissance reverberating beyond its borders? Yes, but not enough, say Baturevych, Lyr and Dovzhyk.

"I think the wave of interest has faded, and Ukrainian writers now face the challenge of competing with global names, especially in so-called 'big' languages," said Baturevych.

Lyr echoed this sentiment: "Ukrainian was in a shadow for so long, there are not enough literary translators to cover the demand."

This struggle of writers to be heard abroad speaks to an entrenched colonial dynamic, argues Dovzhyk. Globally, major publishing houses' appetites for translations of Russian novelists far outweigh those of Ukrainian authors – the "fascination with great imperial Russian culture is the neglect of the cultures of the colonised people".

Baturevych suggests that, particularly in Western Europe, this approach may be a result of the region's own history of colonialism. "Can our point of view be fully understood in languages with an imperial past? It often feels easier for these cultures to resonate with the narratives of another empire rather than the narratives of people who have been fighting for centuries against empires for their very right to exist."

The future of Ukrainian literature

In Russia's war, culture is a battlefield, and Ukrainian writers are both figuratively and literally on the frontlines, fighting for their country's survival and for Ukrainian voices to be heard. As the invasion continues, what will be the future of the country's literature? Ukraine remembers the murder of its writers in Stalin's brutal purges of the 1920s and 1930s as the Executed Renaissance. Only by helping Ukraine to win the war and actively supporting its writers can we ensure that this current literary renaissance does not meet the same fate. ✖

Emily Couch is a contributing editor for Index on Censorship

Can our point of view be fully understood in languages with an imperial past?

In the red zone

A young queer artist in Siberia tells **ALEXANDRA DOMENECH** how his sexuality has been criminalised by the state and how he fears being forcibly conscripted

"I'M ASHAMED TO say this: I'm scared to go outside," said Misha (not his real name), a 25-year-old queer visual artist and photographer, speaking to me over the phone from Siberia.

"It was tough when the war [in Ukraine] began, I felt terrible about it," he said. When Russian President Vladimir Putin announced a military call-up in September 2022, Misha left his homeland for Norway, to take up an artist residency.

But, he explained, he felt lost there. Back home, he had photographed Siberia and its Indigenous people and didn't see how as an artist in exile he could contribute to Norwegian society. Ultimately, he didn't find work and was left with no choice but to return to Russia. He was hoping that going back to his native land would allow him to find meaning in life again and to carry on with his art.

But from the moment he crossed the Russian border, he became aware of a "colossal change" in the atmosphere.

He said "a fear appeared" within him. First and foremost, he was afraid to be persecuted for being gay. In November 2023, just weeks before he returned home, the Supreme Court of Russia labelled "the international LGBT movement" extremist. Since then, places where queer people gather around the country, particularly nightclubs, have been targeted at least 30 times. During some of the raids, the police humiliated and beat men, and collected their personal data.

At least 13 LGBTQ+ extremism

OPPOSITE: LGBTQ+ art has been under siege in Russia – this art exhibit by Index Freedom of Expression Award winner Yulia Tsvetkova in St Petersburg in 2021 could no longer be displayed in the country, and Tsvetkova herself was forced into exile in 2023

criminal cases have now been opened over the past year. In one egregious case last December, Andrei Kotov, who had been allegedly running a travel agency for LGBTQ+ people, died in pretrial detention. Kotov was beaten up, subjected to electric shocks and placed in solitary confinement. He was facing up to eight years in prison if convicted, and his lawyer said he will be tried posthumously. The authorities reported that he had killed himself.

The police have also begun pursuing people just for displaying the rainbow flag which has now been deemed "an extremist symbol". In one case, in the city of Nizhny Novgorod, Anastasia Ershova spent five days in jail for wearing rainbow-coloured earrings.

Another piece of anti-LGBTQ+ legislation passed in 2022 outlawed "gay propaganda". In the city of Ufa, prosecutors used this law to fine a 16-year-old schoolboy for wearing lipstick in a video published on social media. And in Siberia, following a complaint about "LGBT propaganda", a theatre was forced to cancel a children's play, because the role of a princess was played by a man. In July 2023 President Putin added to restrictions on queer and trans people by signing legislation which banned people from medically changing their gender.

As a result of these laws, and the intensifying homophobic and transphobic rhetoric of the government, queer people now face growing threats to their safety. According to a report by LGBTQ+ rights groups Vykhod and Sfera Foundation, 43.5% of LGBTQ+ respondents experienced violence or harassment in 2023, compared to 30% the year before.

Misha told me that when he arrived back in Siberia, the first thing he wanted to do was take off the bright green hat which he wore, to avoid being perceived as queer.

"But I decided that [keeping my hat on] would be my small act of resistance," he said.

But since he has returned, his voice has become deeper, and his manners more stereotypically masculine.

"Nonetheless, I try to assert my [queer] identity the way I can – at the very least, keep my hat on!" he said.

He said that he felt especially exposed in the small city where his parents live because he couldn't "get lost [in the crowd]" there and he didn't feel physically strong enough to defend himself if he were attacked on the street.

He didn't feel this way before the war, when, according to him, LGBTQ+ people were in a "grey zone" where their existence was neither prohibited nor authorised.

"What about now?" I asked. To which he answered: "Now we are in the red zone".

"[Today] I have to hide my [sexual] identity, avoid showing my feminine side and refrain from voicing how I feel about this situation."

He recalled the day a friend, who is gay, took him in his arms in the street and held him, "more than the socially acceptable one-and-a-half seconds".

Misha remembered: "A police car drove by with the headlights on, and so I said [to my friend], '[Stop], I don't want [the officers to ask us] questions'." He didn't want to risk it all for a hug.

He recently came out to his mother and father and, as he predicted, felt rejected by them. He stressed that for his parents, his sexual identity "is simply about sexual preference, or even some deviation from the norm".

This perspective, he added, mirrored the government's narrative.

He said that he hadn't come out on social media because "it could be interpreted as [LGBTQ+] extremism or propaganda" by the authorities.

Misha said he was living in a state of constant fear which has prevented him from feeling inspired to pursue his work; however, he doesn't need to censor his art, as it does not centre around LGBTQ+ politics.

Alongside his fear of punishment for being gay is a fear of conscription.

"When I first arrived here, I was afraid that security forces would knock on my door to take me [to the army office]," Misha recalled.

He decided to stay at a friend's apartment in a modern building, where there were security cameras and a concierge, which he said the police were not able to target as easily. This made him feel safer, albeit not entirely secure.

Since the military draft was announced, civilians have been sent to Ukraine to fight. Police pluck men from the streets, the subway, universities and even bars and dance venues. In November 2024, security forces handed draft notices to men during a raid of a queer nightclub in Moscow.

Misha is scared that one day the authorities will use a centralised database to draft young men like him, who have not yet been called up. A law authorising the implementation of such a system was signed in April 2023.

With this threat looming, he said: "I have to find a way to leave here as soon as I can." ✖

Alexandra Domenech is a Moscow-born, Paris-based journalist

CREDIT: AP Photo / Dmitri Lovetsky

Today I have to hide my sexual identity, avoid showing my feminine side and refrain from voicing how I feel about this situation

Demokratia dismantled

From surveillance of journalists to government corruption, **GEORGIOS SAMARAS** examines how democracy is being eroded in Greece, the very place it was founded

LEFT: Greece, where democracy was born, has been embroiled in a phone-tapping scandal

IN AUGUST 2022, one of the largest surveillance scandals in modern Greek history came to light. Often referred to as the Greek Watergate, it revealed that officials within the government and the National Intelligence Service (EYP), including associates of prime minister Kyriakos Mitsotakis, had been involved in deploying Predator – a spyware tool developed by former Israeli military personnel.

Intellexa, the founding company, had sold multiple licences to the EYP and, according to reports from The Guardian, Reuters and elsewhere, the EYP had subsequently sent messages intended to infect mobile phones and enable electronic surveillance of certain individuals.

Hundreds were targeted, including political opponents of the ruling New Democracy party, journalists, and even government ministers. Among those targeted, the most prominent politician identified was Nikos Androulakis, leader of the Panhellenic Socialist Movement (PASOK) and leader of the opposition.

The Greek government continues to deny ever having purchased or used Predator spyware. On 5 August 2022, during a live television address, Mitsotakis responded to revelations of wiretapping. His inability to provide credible explanations for how the EYP obtained the spyware, combined with his denial of any knowledge of the scandal, heightened suspicions among politicians and journalists. Notably, he had restructured the EYP on the first day of his premiership in 2019, placing it directly under the control of the prime minister's office. Consequently, many questioned how he could have been unaware of such activities.

Nearly three years have passed since the scandal emerged, yet most questions remain unanswered. The prosecutor investigating the case closed the probe last July and refused to further grill individuals linked to the deployment of Predator.

The government allegedly interfered with aspects of the inquiry – including the deliberations of certain committees – and hindered the work of oversight bodies such as the communication security regulator, reported Politico.

Meanwhile, courts have declined to prioritise journalistic and investigative efforts that continue to uncover evidence related to the wiretapping activities.

Unsurprisingly, the government's actions extended beyond covert surveillance. Many people allegedly investigated for their involvement – including Mitsotakis's nephew Grigoris Dimitriadis, the former secretary-general in the prime minister's office – fought back by aggressively pursuing lawsuits against journalists and media outlets investigating the scandal, including Efimerida ton Syntakton and Reporters United.

These weren't just ordinary lawsuits but strategic lawsuits against public participation (Slapps) – deliberately-initiated legal actions aimed at intimidating and silencing critics.

The party filing a Slapp – in this case Dimitriadis – typically does not intend to win the case. The objective is to overwhelm the defendant with legal expenses, fear and exhaustion, ultimately compelling them to cease their reporting or opposition.

Nevertheless, while investigating how the surveillance activities were carried out, Greek journalists managed to uncover something far more significant than they had anticipated – a system that undermines the democratic standards typically upheld by EU member states.

In this regard, Mitsotakis closely resembles Hungary's prime minister Viktor Orbán, who has systematically controlled media organisations by placing them under direct supervision, suppressing criticism and dissent.

Since 2019, corruption has flourished under Mitsotakis's administration and the government appears to have engaged in favouritism and a deliberate dismantling of fundamental human rights – undermining the very foundations of democracy in Greece.

He also allocated funding to the press – both during the Covid-19 pandemic and amid the Ukraine-Russia conflict – in ways that were widely condemned as attempts to financially control specific media outlets.

The funding excluded certain newspapers that were critical of the government, raising concerns about selective support for government-friendly sources, but did include far-right publications affiliated with Kyriakos Velopoulos (an MP known for spreading disinformation) and even non-existent news outlets.

The government has been accused of deploying an extensive network of online trolls on X and TikTok for damage control, including a dedicated war room called Omada Alithias which serves as its mouthpiece. These operations systematically target and suppress dissenting voices, critical media outlets and investigative journalists – particularly those who have exposed the wiretapping scandal – through co-ordinated attacks and gaslighting tactics. These have included downplaying the scandal and dismissing investigative work as fake news.

The impact on press freedom has been dire, with Reporters Without Borders (RSF) confirming some of the worst fears expressed by journalists. In the RSF index, Greece plummeted to 107th position in 2023 before improving somewhat in 2024, rising to 88th. Despite RSF's concerns, Mitsotakis has dismissed the organisation's findings and labelled any criticism of Greece's press freedom as "crap".

Research demonstrates that democratic backsliding invariably begins with media manipulation and the imposition of excessive control – tactics that Mitsotakis has prioritised since the start of his tenure.

The situation in Greece reveals a complex phenomenon, described by Dutch political scientist Matthijs Rooduijn as a "snowball effect". Centrist parties previously perceived as moderate, such as New Democracy, are increasingly cloaking themselves under a liberal façade with the explicit intent of undermining democratic norms.

Instances such as those seen in Greece illustrate that Europe is confronted not only with an existential threat to its democratic institutions but also with the danger of normalising illiberal policies. This troubling trend is underscored by the EU's increasingly permissive approach to surveillance, where the potential consequences are acknowledged yet policy measures remain inadequately implemented.

Additionally, the sustained erosion of press freedoms further exacerbates the vulnerability of democracy. These developments indicate a systemic weakening of safeguards, and the issue is further illustrated by the close and often opaque connections among elected officials which undermine transparency. Without decisive and comprehensive interventions, Europe risks undermining the very foundations that ensure its democratic resilience and integrity.

Greece serves as a prime case study of this troubling trajectory. The country endured a military dictatorship from 1967 to 1974, before democracy was re-established. It has also experienced a serious socio-economic crisis from 2010 to 2019, the subsequent neoliberal restructuring of its economy and a recent resurgence of neo-Nazism. Some of these phases of extreme instability are common in post-authoritarian countries that struggle to uphold the rule of law and democratic principles.

The legacy of the wiretapping scandal cannot be underestimated or overlooked. New Democracy and its successors may attempt to preserve these tools of suppression, potentially leading to further democratic backsliding. Without determined efforts to eliminate such practices, freedom of the press will continue to deteriorate, lacking the legal safeguards needed to prevent unconstitutional measures that can cause long-term damage. ✖

ABOVE: (top): Greece's prime minister Kyriakos Mitsotakis (bottom): Opposition leader Nikos Androulakis was one of the politicians targeted in the "Greek watergate" scandal

Georgios Samaras is an assistant professor of public policy in the School for Government at King's College London

> The legacy of the wiretapping scandal cannot be underestimated or overlooked

Elon Musk's year on X

The tech entrepreneur is now at the heart of the Trump administration.
MARK STIMPSON asks: what has been on his mind this past 12 months?

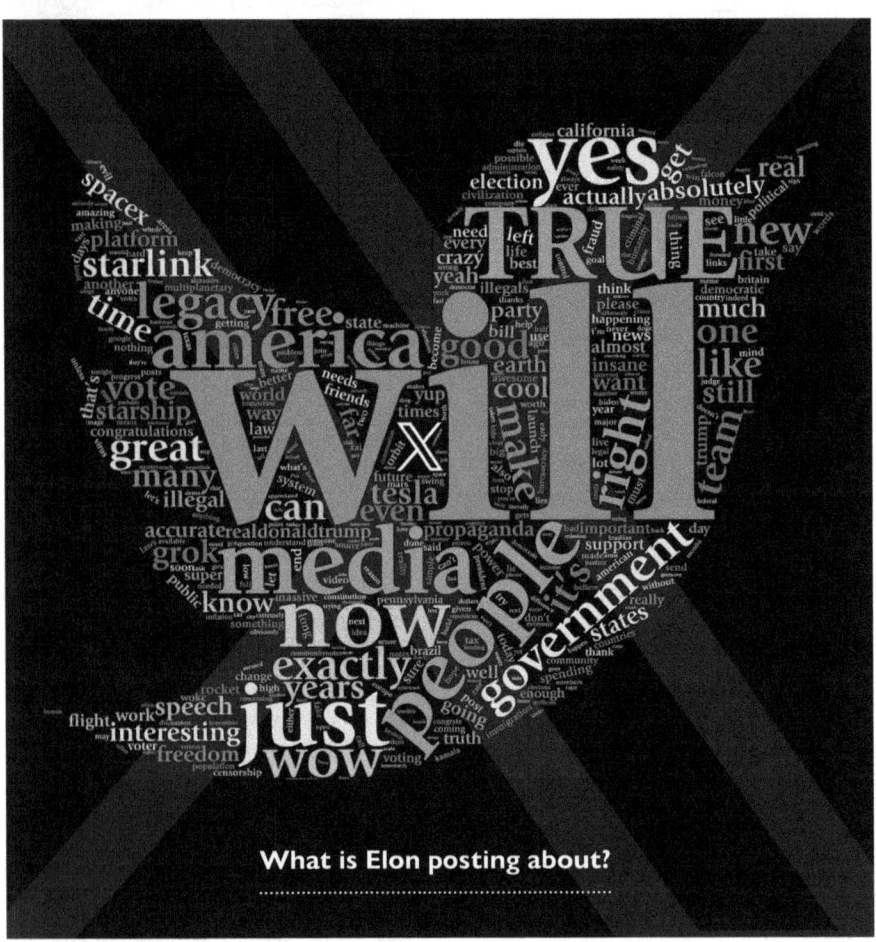

What is Elon posting about?

PEOPLE WAKING UP in Britain on 11 April 1992 were told by The Sun newspaper that it was "The Sun wot won it" after John Major's slim victory in a general election that was expected to go the other way.

Now, a third of a century further on, it is relevant to ask whether it was X wot won it for Donald Trump in the recent US presidential election.

X's owner Elon Musk was certainly on-message in the run-up to the election and he now appears to have been justly rewarded for his support with a wide-ranging role as an adviser and head of the Department of Government Efficiency.

With this in mind, Index decided to analyse what Musk was posting about in the run-up to the election. Musk has always been a power user of X (and previously Twitter), so it was always going to be an interesting analysis.

The analysis covers a year of posts to X between 27 January 2024 and 26 January 2025, a period that spans nine months before the election to just after Trump's inauguration. We chose this period to see both cause and effect.

In that year, Musk made an incredible 12,299 posts to the platform – just over 33 posts a day. Of these, 6,827 are tweets, 5,308 are quoted tweets and 164 retweets.

These posts were seen by other X users more than 77.4 billion times, liked more than 1.3 billion times and retweeted 196,690,378 times, a global influence possibly only matched by the Pope and Lionel Messi.

What is Elon posting about?
This wordcloud (see left) shows what Musk has been posting about most – the larger the word, the more frequently it was mentioned. Some of the words most commonly used in his posts are "will" and "people", often as part of the phrase "will of the people" as in his 6 April 2024 post: "This aggressive censorship appears to violate the law & will of the people of Brazil", referring to a report by the Supreme Court judge Alexandre de Moraes who had dared to block the social media platform in the country.

Musk's companies X, Tesla and Starlink are regularly mentioned in his thousands of posts, as you would expect.

Attacks on what Musk refers to →

 **Musk's posts were retweeted nearly 197 million times, influence possibly only matched by the Pope and Messi**

FEATURES

Who is Elon influenced by?

Circle size shows relative interaction with Musk

Seed/early stage investor at tech VC Sequoia Capital
@Shaunmmaguire

Account of **Visegrad24.com**, a site sharing news on politics, culture wars and tech
@visegrad24

Musk's satellite internet company
@Starlink

Account for the fundraising PAC set up by Elon Musk **@America**

Account featuring citizen journalism on fintech, crypto, AI, longevity, politics
@AutismCapital

Account sharing video clips of Musk run by Belgian writer Jonas Lismont
@ElonClipsX

Tesla Club Silicon Valley
@teslaownersSV

Sawyer Merritt, Tesla investor and EV/space/tech news writer
@SawyerMerritt

Account of an anonymous writer challenging "woke" ideology and legacy institutions
@TheRabbitHole84

Elon Musk
@elonmusk

Cryptocurrency entrepreneur Mario Nawfal **@MarioNawfal**

Account of **Fentasyl.com**, a site aspiring to "discover the hidden truths in public data to advance civil rights, human rights, & victims' rights"
@Fentasyl

Anonymous pro-Trump account using the name Insurrection Barbie
@DefiyantlyFree

Physics engineer and X logo designer Alex Tourville
@Ajtourville

Alex Larusso, political strategist and executive producer on The Benny Show podcast
@Alx

US Senator Rep for Utah Mike Lee
@BasedMikeLee

A UX/UI & graphic designer and crypto influencer working for Dogecoin **@Cb_doge**

Musk's rocket launch company
@SpaceX

Anonymous citizen journalist with pro-Trump and anti-legacy media views
@KanekoaTheGreat

Account sharing Conservative news
@Amuse

Writer and libertarian M Rothmus
@Rothmus

Ian Miles Cheong, co-host of the Other View Podcast
@Stillgray

Anonymous account sharing news on finance, economics and politics
@WallStreetMav

Account "fighting, exposing, and mocking wokeness"
@EndWokeness

Musk's electric vehicle company
@Tesla

Michael Shellenberger, chair of politics, censorship & free speech at University of Austin **@Shellenberger**

INDEXONCENSORSHIP.ORG **37**

By the numbers

12,299

Number of posts to the platform – just over 33 posts a day. Of these, 6,827 are tweets, 5,308 are quoted tweets and 164 retweets

77.4 billion

These posts were seen by other X users more than 77.4 billion times, liked more than 1.3 billion times and retweeted 196,690,378 times

176 Musk's busiest day on the platform was 18 December 2024 when he posted 176 times

→ as the "legacy media" are a common theme throughout the year, with the phrase appearing in 224 posts. These include "An attack by the legacy media in Germany is exactly what I expected and wanted to happen. It will only help the @AfD win" on 10 January 2025. Or "Legacy media is written by the FAR LEFT. Only 3% of journalists are Republican! It is borderline illegal in newsrooms to be a Republican journalist" on 22 December 2024.

Musk has made it abundantly clear what the alternative to the legacy media should be – users of X. His frequently repeated mantra "You are the media now" appeared in 40 posts during the year.

The phrase "free speech" crops up in his posts 40 times during the year, including on 13 March 2024 where he declared "Free speech is the bedrock of democracy" and on 6 September when he said "Kamala wants to destroy your right to free speech under The Constitution". This post was in response to US Daily Mail reporter Charlie Spiering posting on X that Harris had previously said she would use the Department of Justice (DOJ) to "hold social media platforms responsible" for "misinformation".

Who is Elon influenced by?

It is interesting to look at the individuals and accounts that Musk quoted and retweeted during the course of the year. These include:

- GB News (**@GBNEWS**) 13 times including "Elon Musk calls for a 'new election in Britain' as new poll shows Labour's support is plummeting"
- Nigel Farage (**@Nigel_Farage**) seven times including "I questioned whether the Southport attacker was known to authorities and linked to terrorism. Our Deputy Prime Minister accused me of stoking up conspiracy theories. The time has come for @AngelaRayner to apologise."
- Tommy Robinson (**@TRobinsonNewEra**) four times including "ADMIN POST. The UK legacy media are having a meltdown. And of course it's all 'far right' and 'conspiracy theory' jibes. They just don't get it do they? Those buzzwords hold no meaning anymore. We are the media now."

When is Elon posting?

This chart shows when Musk is active on X. The x-axis shows the number of days since the series began, so starting at 26 January 2024 on the left and ending at 25 January 2025 on the right. The y-axis shows the time of day that the post was made (based on the Central Standard Time zone, as Musk is based predominantly in Austin, Texas). This scatter plot shows two things – you can see that Musk is less active between 3am and 9am CST, suggesting that this is when he sleeps. It also shows that he massively ramped up his activity on the platform from around the middle of August 2024, around a month after the official nomination of Donald Trump and J D Vance as the Republican candidates in the presidential election. In the first half of the year, Musk posted on the platform 2,381 times. In the second half of the year, this ramped up to 9,918 times. The day on which Musk posted most often was 18 December 2024, when he posted 176 times. It was the day that a deal was reached on US government spending after president-elect Trump threw his weight behind plans to avoid a government shutdown.

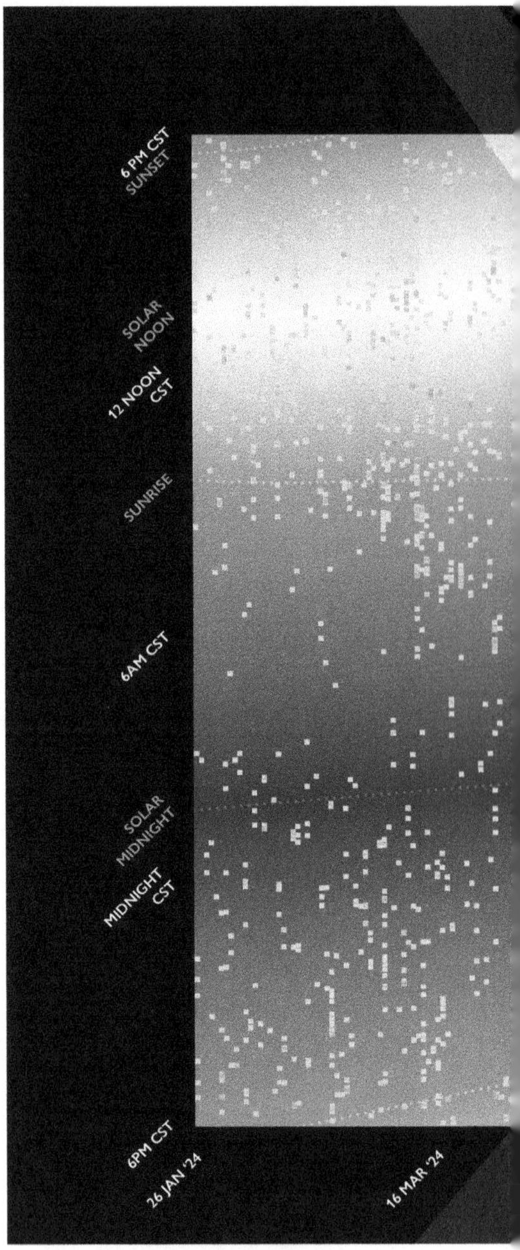

What have we learned?

This analysis is revealing, showing that

Time of day
Tweet heatmap

5 MAY '24 24 JUN '24 13 AUG '24 2 OCT '24 21 NOV '24 10 JAN '25

Musk's focus has been on a limited range of topics – his companies naturally, but also the sort of thinking that has now been confirmed as central to the second Trump presidency. It also reveals the sorts of people that appear to shape Musk's thinking and there are few surprises – crypto fanboys and alt-right conspiracy theorists are front and centre.

Did Musk influence the outcome of the election? His million-dollar prize draws, where he gave away millions to voters in swing states, turned heads and will have converted some to the cause.

Media platforms always like to exaggerate their importance, as in the case of The Sun in 1992.

In November, experts at the Center for Countering Digital Hate issued a report which found that X and Musk's posts played "a central role in enabling the spread of false information about the critical battleground states". On a recent Wired podcast, journalist Tim Marchman said: "The thing that Musk brings above all else is this overwhelming attention vortex. He is constant, he's ubiquitous, he is non-stop, he is pushing 1,000 things at any one time, and he commands attention as the richest man in the world."

This analysis corroborates that. ✖

Mark Stimpson is associate editor at Index on Censorship

ABOVE: Women continue to be part of the protest and resistance movement in Myanmar against the military dictatorship. Here, in the Sagaing region, protesters gather by bike because gathering on foot is too dangerous

Keyboard warriors

Inside and outside Myanmar, female political activists are using the power of the internet to expose the human rights abuses of the military junta, reports **LAURA O'CONNOR**

FOUR YEARS AGO, the military junta in Myanmar overthrew the government in a coup following a national election. While the liberal democratic National League for Democracy won by a landslide, the military alleged widespread fraud, justifying its seizure of power.

Tens of thousands of people took to the streets for mass protests, and the military responded with brutal violence.

Civil defence forces were formed in a huge movement of resistance, including by ethnic minority rebel groups that have fought with the government for decades. Violence has escalated, and the coup continues to claim the lives of thousands of civilians (a conservative estimate) and displace millions more.

In post-coup Myanmar, the internet has become a weapon and the military government has carried out hundreds of internet shutdowns and heavily censored social media in an effort to curb insurgency.

Before 2021, several peace organisations operated in the country, including those advocating for a gender-inclusive process to end the conflict between the government and ethnic armed groups. These include the Alliance for Gender Inclusion in the Peace Process (AGIPP), the Mon Women's Network, and the Gender Equality Network.

But the websites for these organisations are now broken or no longer exist. The women who run them have had to shift their attention towards a more urgent fight to stop the

In Myanmar, everyone has a list of criminal charges. If they want to arrest you, they will always have a reason to do so

widespread sexual and gendered violence being committed by the current regime while attempting to operate within a "digital dictatorship", as labelled by UN human rights experts. Many of these women have fled their home country.

Unable to return to Myanmar, they have built remote digital activism movements, such as the Sisters2Sisters campaign – an online organisation working to build global solidarity for Myanmar's women and orchestrate online campaigns from outside the country. This includes exposing mass sexual violence, often against ethnic minority women and girls, extrajudicial killings of young people, and violence towards other marginalised communities, such as LGBTQ+ groups.

Among the millions of young people who have left the country are Flora and Elle (not their real names), who fled from Myanmar to neighbouring Thailand in 2023. Both worked in gender and youth-focused resistance movements and now do advocacy work from abroad. In order to work within the confines of Myanmar's censorship and Thailand's amenability to the junta, they take refuge in pseudonyms, discreet meeting rooms and virtual private networks (VPNs). I spoke to them both over a joint call, secured via VPN.

Elle, from Sagaing Region, told Index: "Because of the fighting between the resistance forces and the military, the military shuts down the internet intentionally because they don't want [news of] the killings or massacre to spread online."

I first met Elle in Thailand at a meeting about gender-focused advocacy in Myanmar. I asked her about the countless organisations whose websites have been deleted or have stopped posting online.

"[This] is one of the major problems with organisations working on women's rights [and human rights]," she said. "When we publish or announce cases, we have to be aware of the sensitivities of the data and [the danger of] publishing from official websites and social media.

"The Myanmar military has tracked down these posts. They don't target every post but they have a team that specifically looks at data and news from [these] organisations – and if it's within their reach, the [organising] in that township will be shut down."

Flora comes from Kayin State, a district largely populated by Kayin people (also known as Karen people) – an ethnic minority group that has become a hub for the resistance movement and has been targeted by the military since 2021. She herself is Kayin.

"As active [resistance organisation] members, we face a lot of difficulties and challenges," she said. "Because of the internet shutdowns, we don't have internet access, and … the military banned VPNs."

In January this year, the junta passed the Cybersecurity Law which, it claims, aims to "protect and safeguard the sovereignty and stability of the nation from being harmed by cyberthreats, cyberattacks or cyber misuse through the application of electronic technologies".

Within the wide-reaching law is an official ban on unauthorised use of VPNs, with a prison sentence of up to six months and a fine if someone is found with one on their device.

"This impacts every organisation that has supported democracy," Flora explained. "If we use a VPN and they find it on our phones, they will arrest and prosecute us."

Digital access has been a crucial part of the resistance movement, and organisers and protesters have been targeted for digital communications since the February 2021 coup, leading to arrests and shutdowns.

"Look at history," said Flora. →

RIGHT: In the city of Monywa, people blocked the roads with sandbags to prevent the army and police vehicles from entering the town

→ "In 1988, there was no internet and information was locked down. We didn't know what really happened on the ground so it was easy for the government to control information."

That was the year of the 8888 Revolution, which saw youth-led resistance to the government and nationwide protests in support of democracy and human rights. A violent response saw more than 3,000 people killed (with particular cruelty inflicted on ethnic minorities such as the Kayin) and hundreds of thousands displaced. The similarities between today and 1988 show how Myanmar has both a turbulent past and a longstanding legacy of community action.

But Flora said there was a difference between then and now. "Since the beginning, the military has tried to control the internet but the young generations know the effects of technology," she said. "We have VPNs and we have strategies to continue our activities. Youth groups spread knowledge about democracy even with the military trying to cut the internet."

Pro-democracy groups organise largely through encrypted online platforms such as Signal, using VPNs and burner phones. They gain information on the crimes of the junta against civilians, which includes mass

ABOVE: Hubs of activism have developed in Thailand in support of Myanmar's population. In February, activists held a protest opposing the military coup at the Myanmar Embassy in Bangkok

Western governments have shown relatively little outrage at the ongoing abuses

rape and forcing women to become domestic labourers when their husbands have been killed or sent to war.

Platforms such as Sisters2Sisters also continue to publish these crimes and call for the international community to take action.

There is another unexpected way that Myanmar's citizens can continue to communicate freely with the outside world – by using Starlink, the global satellite internet system owned by Elon Musk's SpaceX.

The system is not licensed in Myanmar, but illegal services still operate and Elle and Flora use it to talk to their families back home.

"It's the only way, so there are secret shops for locals – our families go to these shops to call us," said Elle.

In Thailand, safe spaces in Bangkok offer hubs for exiled female activists to reconvene, holding inter-ethnic dialogues and combining the efforts of groups that were previously divided on lines of ethnicity and religion. These conversations, along with communication with groups within Myanmar, have helped to consolidate organising efforts into mass insurgencies of rebel fighters who are continuing to gain ground in Myanmar's jungles.

Digital organising is key to gaining international awareness, and Elle has been working hard to get multilateral bodies to recognise and act on the atrocities.

"No matter how much we are trying to support the rights of women and LGBTQ+ communities, we need support from the international community," she said. Even though the UN has a special mission to Myanmar, Western governments have shown relatively little outrage at the ongoing abuses, and there has been very little military aid for resistance forces.

For campaigners such as Flora and Elle, their activism represents more than a political stance – it's a deeply personal pursuit, with their livelihoods and the safety of their families hinging on it. Their work is fuelled by the hope that by exposing the junta's crimes and continuing to grow insurgency movements, it will pressure global leaders to act and the junta's rule will be shortened.

But even though they are no longer in the country, the new Cybersecurity Law shows that they are increasingly under threat.

"We will be prosecuted because we are working on human rights," said Flora. "If [you] share information against the military, you are criminalised. I am so worried about this. Even if we are outside Myanmar, the law applies to every Myanmar citizen. I am really worried about our activities because access to information is so important."

When asked if they could safely return to Myanmar to visit their families, both of them give painful laughs. "In Myanmar, everyone has a list of criminal charges. If they want to arrest you, they will always have a reason to do so," said Elle.

Within the sanctuary of (relative) freedom in Thailand, Flora and Elle are continuing their movement online.

"We need to know what is happening in Myanmar," said Elle. "Right now, every youth and woman is living in fear because [the junta] restricted the internet … to cover [up] all the injustices." ✘

Laura O'Connor is a freelance writer based in London, largely covering gender and human rights. She was previously based in Delhi, working for a peacebuilding organisation focused on Myanmar, and she now works for an organisation focused on sexual and reproductive rights in West Africa

FEATURES

ABOVE: The abandoned courtyard of Saydnaya prison

Behind the bars of Saydnaya prison

When Bashar al-Assad's regime was overthrown in December, thousands were freed from the dictator's "human slaughterhouse". Reporting from Syria, **LAURA SILVIA BATTAGLIA** speaks to some of the survivors

YOUSIF AND ALAA have never heard of Primo Levi, the Italian-Jewish writer who was imprisoned in Auschwitz concentration camp during the Second World War.

Yet the words coming out of Alaa's mouth while he stands in front of a torture machine and grimaces in disgust and horror sound exactly like lines from Levi's novel The Truce. In the book, Levi describes his own experiences of torture and its effects: "Imagine if this survivor could be called a man."

"Man" in Arabic is "*insan*", although it is better translated as "person" – a human being.

While Alaa forms the noun, *insan*, in his mouth, he points his finger at a hole in the ground: very deep and inhabited by an indistinct pile of rags, bones and congealed blood. Jailers dug this hole in the deepest level of Syria's Saydnaya prison, called the "red section" – the level from which there was no turning back.

This is where some prisoners allegedly ended up, reduced to a pulp of bones and minced meat after being crushed under an enormous hydraulic press. Nearby is "the kitchen", where there are ovens used to make bread for the prison staff. The crushed prisoners were placed on the floor of a room right next door.

Alaa Samah al-Abddallah is 30 years old and spent three of those years detained in Saydnaya prison – the maximum-security detention facility of overthrown Syrian president Bashar al-Assad's regime, termed "the human slaughterhouse".

INDEXONCENSORSHIP.ORG 43

LEFT: Yousif Mahmood al-Salim (left) and Alaa Samah al-Abddallah (right), two former prisoners at Saydnaya, are now able to tell their stories

→ Alaa believes, like many of his cellmates, that this story of a bone-crushing human press is true, "even if none of us has ever seen anything". No prisoner, after all, could have seen it: if that were the case, he could be only a jailer, a torturer. But they all fled before 7 December 2024, leaving 2,000 people – or, as Alaa says, "what remains of what one might call a man" – to emerge from this immense structure.

Insan, again. This word, in this context and from the mouth of a Syrian believer of Islam, evokes the chapter of the same name within the Quran, which is quite explicit on the fate that befalls the wicked in the afterlife.

Yousif, who found himself with Alaa in this hell, also repeats the word again and again when listing the executed – 30,000 between the beginning of the civil war in 2011 and 2018 alone.

And he repeats it when he describes the immorality of the jailers and their brutal methods: beatings with sticks and bundles of barbed wire; electrocutions; collective humiliations; denial of basic needs from food to sleep to personal hygiene; and solitary confinement.

Yousif Mahmood al-Salim has known Alaa since childhood. They are both from Daraa in south-west Syria, and took to the streets in 2011 during the first uprisings. They were arrested more than once and, each time, they emerged from detention even more determined to put an end to the regime.

The last time was three years ago, after deciding to join the jihadist group Al-Nusra, the same group to which the new interim president and rebel leader Ahmed al-Sharaa belonged before founding Hayat Tahrir al-Sham (HTS).

"We found ourselves in here, one day, in this cell. There were 50 people inside," says Yousif.

He drags Alaa into the large prison cell, which is still full of rags, ministerial papers and medical tablets. This is what remains of the personal effects of the freed prisoners and the stench is still unbearable.

He forces Alaa to perform the so-called "train" position when entering and exiting the room. Prisoners were forced to file past each other, holding on to the prisoner in front with one hand, bent over to touch their back with their forehead, and covering their eyes with their shirt so as not to see anything of what was in front, behind and around them.

"In Saydnaya, it was the only way to walk," Yousif says. He appears excited, absorbed in his new role as a "tourist guide" within the former regime's butchery.

Alaa, on the other hand, would have preferred not to return here. He hides his face in the crook of his elbow, not wanting to appear weak.

The pair embrace each other for a long, emotional minute. This dilutes the bitterness of the memory. It is always Yousif who speaks, who interprets Alaa's pain.

"When we recognised each other in the cell, it didn't seem real," he says. "In Saydnaya, we didn't have names – they called us by number. We couldn't speak, so we understood each other with gestures. In prison, the law of absolute silence was in force. Sometimes I think I survived for three years only thanks to Alaa, to his gaze, to his silent friendship."

Here is what remains of a man – *insan*, still – in a place where humanity is denied, if those who survived it can still be called such.

Yousif now shows those who wish to see it the inside of the prison, leading them into the black hole. He also offers his services as a survivor in Marjeh Square in Damascus, especially for families searching for the 150,000 people who disappeared in the system. Alaa tries to make sense of what happened to him by uncovering mass graves in the countryside of Daraa. "I have to bring evidence to international organisations," he says. They both remained in Saydnaya for "only" three years – but now they

 My memory is not strong, and this saved me. It allowed me to put aside the suffering and difficulties experienced in prison

RIGHT: Saydnaya prison, seen from a distance, housed tens of thousands of prisoners who were subjected to abuse and torture

have left, their subconscious always takes them back there.

When I met Salim Hamawi, I asked myself how one could still be alive at 60 after 33 years of imprisonment, 15 of which were in Saydnaya and five in solitary confinement. The other 13 years were spent in other prisons including Lattakia Central Prison on the coast and Adra Prison in Damascus.

Salim is not even Syrian. He is Lebanese and has returned home to the village of Chekka in the province of Batroun. "They arrested me on 3 December 1992 for Santa Barbara," he says, referring to the annual Christian festival celebrated in many parts of the Middle East. "They took me from my home. The reason? I was a member of the Lebanese Forces, the Lebanese Christian militias. But no one ever really told me why I was detained in Syria."

For Salim, these were 33 years of darkness – and literally, during his five years in solitary confinement. The techniques for survival amid such a lack of humanity lie in the little things: a sliver of light that tells you whether it is dawn or dusk, a different food that suggests whether it is dinner or lunch.

"There, I would dream of seeing a little bit of light," he says. "I didn't know my mornings from my evenings. I used to know that it was morning from the food I ate – if I ate an egg or labneh or something like olives then that was the morning, and [it was] the evening if I ate potatoes."

In those hard years, all hope was lost and Salim has now lost faith.

"You certainly wonder why God gave you such a test," he says. "When you stop asking yourself and have accepted, you [either] no longer have faith or you have immense faith."

For Salim, the antidote to inhumanity was to exercise his imagination.

"My memory is not strong, and this saved me. It allowed me to put aside the suffering and difficulties experienced in prison and focus on the life I lived before being arrested, to the point that it became an obsession," he says.

"I started living my freedom in my dreams. I imagined my son growing up and that I had him in front of me. I imagined myself hugging him – living my potential life in my imagination gave me the strength to bear reality."

During his last transfer to the prison in Lattakia, Salim began to write verses. He reads me a beautiful poem dedicated to his wife, Josephine – "the real heroine in this whole story", he says, because she waited for him.

"Love for my wife is my crime/ and my wife is my judge/ she can do what she wants with me/ but you, don't you dare tell her 'I don't love you'."

When he was imprisoned, he missed her more than anything else. "Now, though," – and here Salim looks at an indefinite horizon, losing himself in an unknown whirlpool – "I miss the wall."

At first, I don't understand. He explains patiently and reiterates: "I miss that wall, the wall of my cell. I used to talk to the wall. It was my best friend: I always turn around to look for it."

For Salim, too, there is something that always takes him back there.

There, where he has spent most of his life, he has never been a man. ✖

Laura Silvia Battaglia is a freelance award-winning journalist, living between Italy and Yemen. She has worked in Middle Eastern conflict zones since 2007

ABOVE: Inmates would be forced to march in file with their eyes covered down corridors in Saydnaya, according to prisoner reports

CREDIT: Laura Silvia Battaglia

Painting a truer picture

NATALIE SKOWLUND explores a Colombian city's artistic reckoning, while authorities and tourism threaten to obscure the truth

GUSTAVO PIMIENTA LOST his son, Marcelo, 15 years ago. Time has ticked by, but the wound left after his son was murdered in Medellín, Colombia, may never heal.

"To have to bury a *muchacho* [young man] is very difficult," he said, as he gazed at a photo of Marcelo, who is pictured with his arms slung around his toddler son and a panting dog.

Marcelo, a 23-year-old rapper in the Comuna 13 area of Medellín who went by the nickname MC Chelo, used his music to advocate for peace and an end to violence. He was assassinated in 2010, joining a list of rappers and artists threatened or killed for daring to speak out against the violence and inhumanity they witnessed in this impoverished part of the city.

"He'd say that a child of art is one child fewer in the war," his father told Index.

Medellín, one of Colombia's largest cities, was once considered the "murder capital of the world" due to drug-fuelled conflict. Comuna 13 suffered particularly high rates of violence due to its prime location along a drug trafficking route.

A controversial 2002 state military campaign, Operation Orión, aimed to take back control of Comuna 13 from guerrilla groups. The operation and its aftermath resulted in hundreds of civilians being forcibly disappeared.

Locals insisted for decades that the remains of their loved ones were hidden in La Escombrera – literally "the dump". Mothers searched for their children, calling for justice with little attention from authorities.

In the years after Operation Orión, Comuna 13 began to see a boom in artistic expression. Seta Fuerte, a graffiti artist from Bogotá, arrived about a decade after Orión during what he called a hopeful "springtime" in Medellín.

"People started to paint, they started to rap, and they started to dress however they wanted," the artist, who asked to use only his alias due to potential safety threats, told Index.

Art became a way to reflect local memories and tell truths that challenged the status quo. But illustrating the area's tragic stories wasn't easy.

"There isn't a single home in this area that doesn't have any dead," he said. "You'd come, you'd paint, and every day you'd return home with a broken heart."

Creating art also put people at risk. Between 2009 to 2012, 10 rappers from Comuna 13 were assassinated, and visual artists were no safer.

"Me and almost all graffiti artists have had a gun to the head at some point," Seta Fuerte said. "Depending on what you say and how you go about it, you can also risk your life."

Over time, life began to improve in the commune. In 2011, the government invested in outdoor escalators to help people get up and down the area's steep hills, and local street art began to attract interest from outsiders.

Groups of tourists arrived – in trickles at first, and then in hordes. Tour guides explained the stories behind the art and the political context, also selling a message of transformation and rebirth in the commune, aligned with the identity Medellín sought as a city.

But as the years passed, murals faded and narratives changed. New art replaced the old, and with it subtle changes in the tenor and messaging. Where early street art often depicted allusions to its violent past, new art

ABOVE: Murals began to emerge in Medellín's Comuna 13, dealing with painful events in the city

began to focus on diluted scenes of animals and nature.

As tourist numbers began to rocket, local gangs took notice and began to

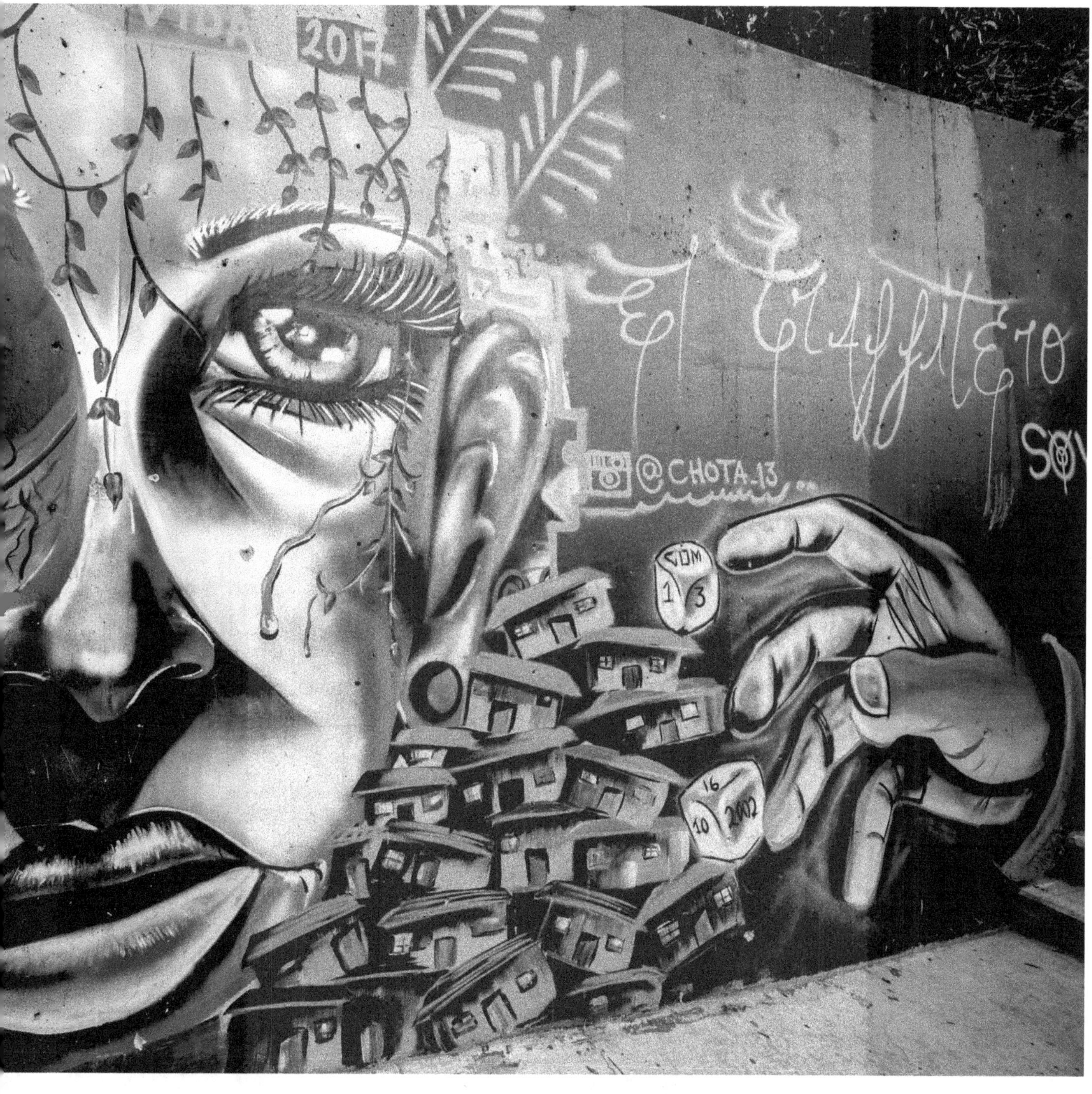

CREDIT: John Seagle / Alamy

extort tour guides, artists and vendors, and manoeuvre drugs and child sex trafficking not far from the tourists. Kiosks were set up to cater to tourists' whims for Pablo Escobar T-shirts and cheap beer, often obscuring the murals that had once been the reason to visit.

"It worries me that at some point it will have lost the spirit from which it all began," Seta Fuerte said. "That the important stories will stop being told, that it will become merely decorative – that the memories will be lost." But the truth will be set free. →

Almost all graffiti artists have had a gun to the head at some point

LEFT: Street art in Comuna 13 soon fell victim to commercialisation, with the meaning behind the artwork obscured in place of more palatable messages, as seen here in 2024

There isn't a single home in this area that doesn't have any dead

→ Last December, the first human remains were exhumed from La Escombrera. Bodies recovered included those of a 20-year-old woman who led a youth sports group and a 28-year-old disabled man who worked as a street vendor.

In January, graffiti artists, victims and activists took to the streets in Medellín to paint a new mural reflecting the recent exhumations in La Escombrera, including, in bold yellow letters, the phrase "*Las cuchas tenían razón*" ("The old ladies were right").

The mothers who'd long pointed to the dump as the burial site of their loved ones had finally been proven correct – two decades after their search began.

A day after the mural was completed, a plain grey wall stood in its place. Medellín's mayor Federico Gutiérrez had told workers to paint over it, reasoning that the mural's creators were seeking to foment hate and political division.

But the message was not suppressed for long. Activists and artists soon returned to paint the mural again, this time much larger. In cities across Colombia and around the world, others took to the streets to re-create the mural or paint related messages, and the phenomenon began to appear across social media.

Max Yuri Gil Ramírez, director of the Institute of Political Studies at the University of Antioquia and a former member of Colombia's Truth Commission, said there was some irony in the city's initial decision to erase the mural and its loaded message.

"Sometimes attempts to make a memory invisible propel it to spread further and become more ingrained," he said. "There can't be an 'official' memory – there shouldn't be an official memory. There must be many memories, multiple memories."

Gustavo Pimienta, the father whose son died in 2010, said there's no question as to why art like that must be protected and preserved.

"So that the people remember, *madrecita* [my dear]," he said. "So that the people remember." ✖

Natalie Skowlund is a freelance journalist based in Colombia and the USA

54(01):46/48|DOI:10.1177/03064220251332625

RIGHT: Artists take part in painting the Digging the Truth mural in January 2025 after a similar one was erased by authorities

FEATURES

The reporting black hole

FASIL AREGAY speaks to journalists who are no longer able to cover news freely or safely in Ethiopia

IT HAS BEEN nearly four years since Abrehet was detained by Ethiopia's authorities for reporting on the 2021 Tigray civil war. Now the war has ended she has managed to leave the country, and fast-paced news cycles have overshadowed the atrocities committed during the two-year conflict between the Tigray region and the federal government.

But the threats and abuses Abrehet faced during her two-month detention on charges of receiving and disseminating false information from a terrorist group, have haunted her ever since.

"I'm traumatised," she said, requesting anonymity for fear that speaking out could endanger her family back home. Even from afar, she cautiously shares details of her ordeal that won't risk her being identified.

"Police took me and my colleagues to a detention centre in the Afar region, about 210km from Addis Ababa. The conditions were terrifying."

For 35 days, her whereabouts were unknown to her family. She was denied a lawyer.

"I wasn't given sanitary pads or spare clothes, and I survived on one piece of bread a day, which caused chronic heartburn," she recalled.

Abrehet is one of many Ethiopian journalists who have faced harassment, arrest and exile. According to the Committee to Protect Journalists (CPJ), at least 54 journalists and media workers have fled Ethiopia since 2020.

Only two years before, when Ethiopia's new Prime Minister Abiy Ahmed took office in 2018, the country was optimistic that media freedom was being restored. He released jailed reporters and lifted bans on over 260 outlets. But as Ethiopia descended into inter-ethnic conflict and civil war, press freedoms collapsed.

ABOVE: A protest in London against the Ethiopian government on 10 November 2024. Demonstrators condemn human rights abuses in the Amhara region of Ethiopia, and demand the release of imprisoned journalists

Abrehet said her ordeal began in June 2021.

"I was in the newsroom preparing the news when armed federal police stormed in, ordered everyone to raise their hands, and searched the office," she said. "They took us to the Federal Crime Investigation Bureau before transferring us to Awash 7 Kilo Detention Centre."

She said that authorities branded journalists reporting on the conflict – both Tigrayan and non-Tigrayan – as "junta", a term used for Tigray People's Liberation Front (TPLF) supporters.

"At one point, an officer pulled out a gun with 30 bullets and said that was enough to finish us all," she recalled.

After her release, fear kept her from resuming journalism. Only after leaving Ethiopia seven months ago was she able to report again – from exile.

Mundane reports only

Belete Kassa, an independent journalist, →

 An officer pulled out a gun with 30 bullets and said that was enough to finish us all

CREDIT: Joao Daniel Pereira/ZUMA Press Wire

INDEXONCENSORSHIP.ORG **49**

Only the parks and street lights the prime minister has built can be reported on

→ co-founded media outlet Ethio News in 2021 to cover the war that killed an estimated 600,000 people and saw the government accused of war crimes. It put him on the authorities' radar.

"In 2021, our office was broken into and our equipment was stolen. We believe government forces were responsible," Kassa said from exile. His colleague Belaye Manaye, co-founder of Ethio News, was arrested in November 2023. When Kassa learned he was also being pursued, he went into hiding. After his home was raided, he fled Ethiopia in December 2023, as federal forces clashed with the Fano armed group in the Amhara region.

"The media is completely shut down in Ethiopia," he said. "Journalists can't work independently. First, Tigrayan reporters were targeted, then those covering the Oromo conflict, and later those reporting on the Amhara war. The government systematically closed media outlets to silence reports on human rights abuses, rapes and war crimes."

He added: "Only the parks and street lights the prime minister has built can be reported on."

A 2024 CPJ report highlights how Ethiopia's restrictive laws and its media regulator, the Ethiopian Media Authority (EMA), have suppressed press freedom. Journalists have been repeatedly imprisoned, facing charges under laws against hate speech, disinformation, and "outrages against the constitution" – an offence that carries the death penalty.

Kassa now reports on Ethiopia from exile, but it's an uphill battle.

"Being far from the community makes gathering information difficult. Immigration challenges, the emotional toll of separation from family and high phone and internet costs add to the struggle," he said.

Still, he believes exiled journalists have played a crucial role.

"We've managed to raise awareness and share information with international media and advocacy groups," he said.

A difficult decision

Meaza Mohammed, a broadcast journalist, has been imprisoned three times. Despite the risks, she always returned to Ethiopia – until August 2023. That month, fighting erupted in Amhara, and the government declared a nationwide state of emergency.

"Almost all my colleagues – journalists, activists and politicians – were arrested. Many are still missing," Mohammed said. She had left in July to attend a function in the USA. "It became clear that if I returned, I would either be imprisoned again or even killed."

Mohammed believed that the crackdown has gone beyond targeting independent journalists.

"The government isn't just targeting individuals for their work, but also for their identity. Being both an independent journalist and Amhara made me an obvious target," she said. She has been in exile since then.

The conflict between the federal army and Fano militias – former allies against the TPLF – escalated after the government moved to disarm them. Once again, civilians bore the brunt of the violence. But this time, independent journalists weren't there to cover it.

Mohammed continues to report via YouTube but faces multiple hurdles.

"Staying connected to the realities on the ground is one of the biggest challenges. Before, I would speak directly with victims. Now, the government's crackdown has created an information blackout," she said.

Fear and censorship have deterred sources from speaking.

"Many of my contacts are either imprisoned, in hiding or too scared to communicate due to surveillance," she said.

Exiled journalists also struggle with credibility.

"The government labels us as foreign agents and accuses us of spreading misinformation," she said. Financial constraints make matters worse: "There's little funding or support."

Then there's the personal toll. "The constant fear for your family back home never goes away," Mohammed said. "But we keep going."

The reality for those who stay

Mikiyas Tilahun, a former Reyot Media reporter, has neither fled nor given up on journalism. But staying in Ethiopia comes at a cost.

"I was detained for six months in Bahir Dar Prison in 2021, without charges," he said. "The police assaulted me when they arrested me."

Despite the trauma, he eventually returned to the newsroom. But self-censorship is now a necessity.

"I continue working, but under extreme caution," he said.

Kassa, the Ethio News journalist, sees little hope for improvement. "It's not just the media that's under attack – civic and democratic organisations are being shut down too," he said. "Recently, five civic groups were closed, and others are under threat. This isn't an environment where journalism can survive."

Polarisation has made neutrality nearly impossible. He added: "There's no middle ground for journalists anymore." ✖

Fasil Aregay is an investigative journalist in Ethiopia who is published in multiple local outlets

This piece is published in collaboration with Egab, an organisation working with journalists across the Middle East and Africa

SPECIAL REPORT

— THE FORGOTTEN PATIENTS —

"Foreign aid is not distributed properly, and most of it goes to specific Taliban-affiliated groups. Ordinary people, especially women and children, are deprived of this aid."

NOWHERE TO TURN | ZAHRA JOYA | P.84

SPECIAL REPORT ◆ THE FORGOTTEN PATIENTS

Whistleblowing in an empty room

MARTIN BRIGHT investigates the culture of secrecy shrouding maternity services and women's healthcare in England

IN OCTOBER 2022, Dr Bill Kirkup, who was responsible for undertaking investigations into maternity scandals at hospitals in the north-west and south-east of England, wrote an open letter to the UK health and social care secretary and the chief executive of the National Health Service quoting a bereaved mother: "When your baby dies, it's like someone has shut the curtains on life, and everything moves from colour to darkness."

Kirkup continued: "How much more difficult must it be if the death need not have happened? If similar deaths had occurred previously but had been ignored? If the circumstances of your baby's death were not examined openly and honestly, leaving the inevitability of future recurrence hanging in the air?"

His words were meant to draw a line under the scandals, but they proved horribly prophetic. Kirkup was recently called to give evidence at the inquest into the death of Ida Lock, who was resuscitated after birth at the Royal Lancaster Infirmary in November 2019 but died a week later from brain injuries sustained during delivery due to a lack of oxygen.

The hospital, part of the University Hospitals of Morecambe Bay NHS Foundation Trust (UHMBT), initially denied any failings but was ultimately forced to recognise that mistakes had yet again been made. A whistleblower came forward in February to claim that warnings had not been heeded, causing the inquest to be delayed.

The whistleblower, former inspector Ian Kemp, claimed health watchdog the Care Quality Commission (CQC) "watered down" his report after he was asked to investigate maternity care at the NHS trust following the death of baby Ida. At the time, the CQC's lawyers told the coroner's court the allegations were "not recognised" by the watchdog.

The five-week inquest has now finished, with coroner Dr James Adeley concluding that Ida's death was caused by the "gross failure" of three midwives to "provide basic medical care". In a statement, Tabetha Darmon, chief nursing officer at UHMBT, said: "Losing a child is tragic and our heartfelt condolences go out to Ida's parents, family and loved ones. We are truly sorry for the distress we have caused. We accept that we failed Ida and her family and if we had done some things differently and sooner, Ida would still be here today." She also apologised for "the way investigations into Ida's death have been conducted since 2019", adding that the trust takes the coroner's conclusions "very seriously", and it will "do everything [it] can to prevent this from happening to another family".

Recent scandals that have blighted UK hospitals reveal a horrific pattern of cover-up and secrecy in the NHS. Time and time again, concerns over the treatment of the most vulnerable in society – babies and women in particular – have been silenced or ignored by senior managers and clinicians.

"A series of failures at almost every level"

The investigation into the UHMBT in 2015 found that 11 babies and one mother died at Furness General Hospital between 2004 and 2013 as a result of failures in clinical competence, poor working relationships between medical staff and a resistance to investigating serious incidents. Kirkup concluded: "Our findings are stark and catalogue a series of failures at almost every level – from the maternity unit to those responsible for regulating and monitoring the trust."

Published seven years later in October 2022, the report of the investigation into East Kent Hospitals University NHS Foundation Trust found that 45 babies had lost their lives due to failures of teamwork, professionalism, compassion and listening, noting a resistance to listening to parents' concerns. Kirkup wrote: "It is too late to pretend that this is just another one-off, isolated failure, a freak event that 'will never happen again'."

Meanwhile, an unprecedented review of cases at the Shrewsbury and Telford Hospital NHS Trust spanning two decades was also published in 2022 and found that more than 200 babies and nine mothers died unnecessarily. The chair of the review, senior midwife Donna Ockenden, said her report was "about an NHS maternity service

RIGHT: A poster in Westminster encourages NHS workers to speak up about wrongdoing and inadequate care they see happening in their trusts

> **When your baby dies, it's like someone has shut the curtains on life, and everything moves from colour to darkness**

LEFT: A lack of protections for NHS whistleblowers, both staff and patients, is stopping them from being able to speak out without fear of retribution

Systemic issues in maternity care

The inquiries that have already published their reports identified a common set of problems with senior clinicians and hospital managers failing to listen to parents or to act when the alarm was raised by staff. We wait to see if Nottingham will be any different, though the NHS's track record invites scepticism. This is not a historical story; it is an ongoing crisis with new details and new scandals emerging all the time.

Maxwell Mclean, the former chair of Bradford Teaching Hospitals NHS Foundation Trust, is currently pursuing an employment tribunal over unfair dismissal, claiming the trust was unhappy after he raised concerns about baby deaths in 2021. Meanwhile, a review into baby deaths at University Hospitals of Derby and Burton NHS Foundation Trust published its report in 2024, finding that national guidelines for monitoring foetal movements had not been followed and identifying "care issues" that could have contributed to loss of life in 150 cases.

Some parents want a full national inquiry into maternity services. Neil and Katie Russell, whose baby Poppy died in April 2021 at The Princess Royal Hospital in Telford, have called for a nationwide investigation and have been joined by other bereaved parents from across the country. The Russells believed the increased scrutiny on the Telford hospital would mean their baby would be safe, but she died while the Ockenden inquiry was being carried out. In 2023, a coroner ruled that Poppy's death was preventable and said effective

that failed. It failed to investigate, failed to learn and failed to improve, and therefore often failed to safeguard mothers and their babies at one of the most important times in their lives".

Speaking to Index, Ockenden said there was an immediate need for investment in perinatal services (the period of time between becoming pregnant and up to a year after giving birth) – but this is not the whole story. "There has to be an absolute commitment to listening to women, hearing women and acting on what they tell you," she said. "It's fair to say that for many staff in the NHS, not just maternity, they do not currently have the time to care. But there are occasions when there would be time and still women aren't listened to."

She is now carrying out a review into maternity services at the Nottingham University Hospitals NHS Trust, which will examine more than 2,500 cases of death or serious harm in the maternity unit over a 10-year period from 2012 to 2022. Her inquiry, which had been due to report at the end of this year, will be extended until June 2026 after 300 new cases were discovered by a coroner.

Even staff at Nottingham University Hospitals NHS Trust were not necessarily protected when they chose to have their babies delivered by their colleagues. Jack Hawkins, who worked as a doctor at the trust, and his wife Sarah, who was employed there as a senior physiotherapist, lost their daughter Harriet in 2016 when she was stillborn. The trust admitted that a series of errors by midwives and doctors had led to Harriet dying in the womb and agreed to a £2.8 million payout (roughly $3.6 million) in 2021. The couple are now at the centre of the campaign for justice for families affected by the Nottingham scandal and have called for full transparency and accountability.

 **It is too late to pretend that this is just another one-off, isolated failure, a freak event that "will never happen again"**

monitoring of her foetal heart rate had not happened.

In May 2024, the UK's All-Party Parliamentary Group (APPG) on Birth Trauma published its report Listen to Mums: Ending the Postcode Lottery in Perinatal Care. It recommended the creation of a maternity commissioner post, who would report directly to the prime minister and develop a national maternity improvement strategy.

Four months later, the CQC reported that harm at maternity units was at risk of becoming normalised following a review of 131 units across England. The pattern of criticism was familiar: staffing shortages, problems with equipment, cramped wards, inconsistencies in reporting incidents and poor leadership and management leading to a blame culture. Mothers and babies from ethnic minority backgrounds were found to be at increased risk, with a lack of support for women whose first language was not English.

The maternity units investigated by the CQC had not been inspected since 2021. They amounted to two-thirds of the total number of units in the country – and of those, nearly half were rated inadequate or in need of improvement and 65% were judged to be failing on the single issue of safety.

Threatened for speaking out

The investigations carried out by Kirkup and Ockenden and the recent CQC review build a picture of a systemic failure in maternity services across the country. But this is often compounded by a culture of secrecy, cover-up and blame.

And this is not confined to maternity services. It is no coincidence that NHS trusts repeatedly found to be dysfunctional often have a record of silencing those trying to raise the alarm.

RIGHT: An inquest into the death of baby Ida Lock, who sustained brain injuries during delivery at the Royal Lancaster Infirmary, concluded in March

It is helpful to look at the problems faced by the NHS as either horizontal or vertical. The horizontal problems are those facing services in particular areas of care, such as for older people, breast screening or maternity. But then there are the vertical problems faced by a specific NHS trust, where both professionals and patients claim a toxic culture runs from top to bottom.

Radiographer Sue Allison claimed she was bullied, ostracised and blocked from promotion after raising concerns in 2012 about malpractice in the breast screening unit at Royal Lancaster Infirmary (part of UHMBT) and cancer diagnoses being missed. Instead of addressing the potentially fatal consequences of failures in the hospital's breast screening unit, Allison claims managers victimised her for blowing the whistle and eventually forced her to resign and abandon the career she loved.

Allison later successfully challenged the gagging order she had felt pressured to sign, and in 2019 health secretary Matt Hancock used her case to propose a ban on the use of non-disclosure agreements in the NHS.

Speaking at the time to The Daily Telegraph, Hancock said: "We stand with whistleblowers. Making someone choose between the job they love and speaking the truth to keep patients safe is an injustice I am determined to end." Six years later, this ban is yet to be enforced.

Allison told Index that UHMBT later offered her an advisory job working with the director of nursing, but she turned it down because of the confidentiality clause contained in the contract. Instead, she successfully stood for election as a public governor of the trust. According to government guidance, the holder of this role "represents the public's interests and works to ensure that an organisation meets the needs of its community". However, Allison claims that when she and two other governors began to hold the trust to account, they were sidelined and eventually forced out.

Allison told Index: "Some trusts just have a toxic culture. After more than 30 years of service as a radiographer, I saw my career destroyed because I tried to raise the alarm about potential serious harm to women in the care of the Morecambe Bay trust.

"My subsequent attempts to hold the trust to account over the following 10 years were frustrated because the institution did not genuinely believe in transparency and was determined to protect its reputation, even to the detriment of the patients it had a duty to care for and protect."

→ At the time of her resignation in 2023, UHMBT chair Mike Thomas was reported as saying: "We respect Sue's decision to stand down as a trust governor and thank her for her contribution… during her time on our Council of Governors." He offered Allison an exit interview to discuss further issues.

"We wish to make it clear that bullying and/or harassment has absolutely no place within our trust. All feedback and concerns are taken seriously and we actively work to improve on any issues raised," he added.

Not all whistleblowers are staff, and Allison has supported patients putting their heads above the parapet. One of these cases is Diana Merrick, who had surgery at Westmorland General Hospital (also part of UHMBT) after treatment for breast cancer.

Merrick, an artist from Cumbria, alleges that the routine operation she was booked in for was changed to a more complex one at the last minute. Following the surgery, she developed complications and raised concerns but claims these were ignored. Five months later, she had to have an emergency operation and is now waiting for breast reconstructive surgery.

She says she was characterised as "anxious", "demanding" and a "serial complainer". She has complained to UHMBT, the General Medical Council (GMC) and the Parliamentary and Health Service Ombudsman.

She told Index: "If the trust continues to dismiss legitimate concerns, patient safety will suffer, and preventable deaths will continue. I initially raised concerns on the advice of a staff member, solely to help the hospital and protect others from harm. I was shocked when the hospital responded with contempt and tried to silence me."

Index put Merrick's claims to UHMBT but the trust was unable to respond by the time of publication for reasons of patient confidentiality.

Another case that Allison championed was that of Peter Duffy, a consultant surgeon in urology at UHMBT. In 2015, Duffy had blown the whistle to the CQC about dangerous practices within UHMBT's urology services, which had led to 520 cases of serious harm. NHS England ended up commissioning an investigation into the department.

The trust was later forced to pay out £102,000 (roughly $132,000) in damages to Duffy for constructive

> There are many reasons why people may feel reluctant to speak up in any industry. For example, they may be concerned they will be seen as disloyal, a "snitch" or a troublemaker

dismissal. In 2023, the surgeon announced he would be leaving the medical profession entirely after 43 years of service as a result of being "hunted" out of the NHS.

Tommy Greene has tracked the whistleblowing cases at UHMBT, first as a local reporter with The Westmorland Gazette and then as a journalist with Computer Weekly, the publication which broke the story of the Post Office IT scandal.

He told Index: "A culture of secrecy and cover-up appears to have persisted at the Morecambe Bay trust well after the revelations of its historic maternity scandal came to light. There is no doubt this has contributed to the trust's ongoing problems, which show little sign of going away.

"Over the last decade, it has become clear that similar practices to those previously uncovered at the trust's maternity services – burying evidence of healthcare failings, poor clinical governance and reprisals against multiple whistleblowers – have led to further serious harms across several more departments, including Morecambe Bay's breast screening, urology, and trauma and orthopaedics units.

"Disproportionate focus on reputation management – in particular, on advancing a 'turnaround' narrative at UHMBT – has led to avoidable suffering for patients and families, the trashing of various careers and an overall loss of public confidence in the management

LEFT: (Left to right) Medical doctor Shoo Lee, politician Sir David Davis and human rights lawyer Mark McDonald at a press conference presenting new evidence in defence of Lucy Letby

of local healthcare services. Far from promoting the NHS's stated 'freedom to speak up' values, these episodes are likely to have a chilling effect on workers who are keeping the service going at a time of unprecedented pressure."

Looking to the future

The case of Lucy Letby, the nurse convicted of murdering seven babies at the Countess of Chester Hospital and attempting to kill six more, has brought whistleblowers in the NHS into sharp focus. Doubt has been cast on the safety of the convictions by an independent panel of experts put together by Letby's solicitors. But what is not in doubt is that between June 2015 and June 2016, babies were harmed and died unnecessarily, just as they did in scandals at other hospitals around the country.

A judicial inquiry into the case is being carried out by Lady Justice Thirlwall, who will report in the autumn. The former chairman of the Countess of Chester Hospital NHS Foundation Trust, Sir Duncan Nichol, has already admitted the hospital "failed to keep babies safe in their care" and has apologised, recognising that failures caused "unimaginable grief for the families whose babies died".

The whistleblowing charity Protect recently estimated that the cost of the Letby case, including the Thirlwall Inquiry and estimated compensation to the bereaved families, is likely to run to £40 million (roughly $50 million). In a report which also looked at the Post Office scandal and the collapse of construction company Carillion, the charity made a series of recommendations. These included placing a duty on employers to investigate whistleblowers' concerns, increasing whistleblower protection to everyone in the workplace, addressing the consistent failures at board level and ensuring implementation of recommendations from inquiries.

The government is already looking at stronger protections for NHS whistleblowers, including proposals to ban managers who silence whistleblowers from working in the NHS and to make them accountable for responding to patient safety concerns. The recent decision to scrap NHS England could also provide an opportunity to increase transparency through organisational restructure.

It is clear that policy change would help. However, in many cases the whistleblowers leading the campaigns for justice are the bereaved parents themselves and no amount of workplace protections would ensure their voices were heard.

What frustrates campaigners is that many of the statutory frameworks are already in place. The NHS regulator, the CQC, is there to ensure individual trusts are doing their jobs. It is now 10 years since Sir Robert Francis QC published his Freedom to Speak Up review into whistleblowing in the NHS. This led to the establishment of the National Guardian's Office and the creation of Freedom to Speak Up Guardians. There are now 1,200 guardians whose job is to encourage a culture of openness free from fear of reprisals from managers.

One paragraph in Francis's report still stands out: "There are many reasons why people may feel reluctant to speak up in any industry. For example, they may be concerned they will be seen as disloyal, a 'snitch' or a troublemaker. Two particular factors stood out from the evidence we gathered: fear of the repercussions that speaking up would have for an individual and for their career; and the futility of raising a concern because nothing would be done about it."

Beyond the questions of transparency and accountability lies the fundamental problem of resourcing – in many hospitals there are simply not enough obstetricians and midwives. The various reviews into baby deaths have also revealed a lack of specialist training and an almost cult-like obsession with "natural" childbirth.

But none of this explains the other consistent findings of these reports: the poor communication between health professionals, the failure to learn from past mistakes, and the lapses in oversight. And nothing excuses the most damning judgment that haunts each of these maternity scandals: the lack of compassion for the parents who just wanted to know why their baby had died. ✖

Martin Bright is editor-at-large at Index on Censorship

ABOVE: Members of the media outside the Countess of Chester Hospital, where convicted murderer Lucy Letby worked

SPECIAL REPORT ♦ THE FORGOTTEN PATIENTS

An epidemic of corruption

DANSON KAHYANA paints a picture of healthcare in Uganda: a two-tier approach, obscured by silence

NEARLY EVERYBODY IS scared of talking about the mess in Uganda's health sector. Several doctors and health officers gave me details of the tragic deterioration of the sector over the years, but none of them would speak on the record because they feared that they would be swiftly punished if they did.

In Uganda's political landscape at the beginning of 2025, censorship in the health sector thrives. Everybody – including politicians who belong to the ruling party – has been silenced by the powerful family running the country: Gen Yoweri Kaguta Museveni, the president and commander-in-chief (who has been in power since 1986) and his son, Gen Muhoozi Kainerugaba, who has been the commander of the defence forces since March 2024.

These two broadcast the power they have from the rooftops. Time and again, Museveni has said he would crush his enemies (meaning his political opponents), while his son has informed the world that his wish is to behead opposition politician Robert Kyagulanyi Ssentamu (popularly known by his stage name Bobi Wine) and hang retired colonel Kizza Besigye, who was abducted in November 2024 from Kenya and has been imprisoned in Uganda ever since. Besigye was at one time Museveni's personal doctor before becoming an opposition leader.

When members of parliament demanded that Kainerugaba appear before them to explain his controversial statements (usually made on X), he refused, declaring them clowns and threatening to arrest them. He has done all this with impunity, aware that nobody dare touch him.

It is common knowledge that Uganda's health sector is in a sorry state following four decades of misrule. There is the theft of public funds; appointments and promotions of medical personnel based more on regional, ethnic and political affiliation than on merit; and the prioritisation of political projects over essential ones.

An issue underlined by those I spoke to was the difficulty in accessing facilities because of long distances between health centres, a lack of essential medicines and the high cost of medical services, and low doctor-patient and nurse-patient ratios of approximately one to 25,000 and one to 11,000 respectively. They also pointed out the lack of regulation of the pharmaceutical industry, leading to an increase in fake medicines, drugs being sold over the counter – including antibiotics – and the poor training of medical staff in under-staffed, ill-equipped and inefficiently-monitored universities and colleges.

Olive Kobusingye, a surgeon and researcher, explained the state of censorship in the health sector. She told me about the ways in which it manifests itself, how it imperils the provision of health services and the impact it has on Ugandans in general, particularly the marginalised ones who cannot afford to fly out of the country for specialised treatment the way ruling party politicians and senior civil servants do.

Kobusingye has published more than 80 articles in peer-reviewed journals and two books on Uganda, both documenting the heroism of ordinary Ugandans under Museveni.

She emphasised the climate of fear in which medical personnel work. She said they could not speak openly about glaring inadequacies, inefficiencies and inequalities in the health sector because they feared being punished – for example, by being disciplined, denied promotion or transferred to remote areas of the country.

"This fear leads to widespread

ABOVE: Olive Kobusingye is one of very few who have spoken out publicly about corruption within Ugandan healthcare

> They could not speak openly about glaring inadequacies, inefficiencies and inequalities in the health sector because they feared being punished

self-censorship, which makes medical officers look on as the health sector deteriorates," she said.

Because the government is not held accountable, many communities – especially those in rural areas – consider healthcare a privilege and not a right.

"For such marginalised communities, whatever bare minimum they get from the government, for instance a health centre that is poorly stocked and staffed, is good enough," Kobusingye explained.

It is common knowledge in the country that any attempt to educate people about their rights is frustrated by the state, which then paints the educator in question as an agent provocateur. Such a person faces arrest on some trumped-up charge of fomenting trouble or engaging in hate speech, which is the new standard charge slapped on people who call out the government. This fear of arrest leaves the state narrative intact: that despite a few shortages here and there, there is no crisis in the health sector – everything is under control.

But there is a lot that demonstrates that all is not well. Consider the more than $397 million earmarked for building a hospital in Lubowa. It should be operational by now, but there is nothing to show for it. All efforts by parliament to access the construction site have been blocked, and it is no wonder that Kobusingye considers Uganda's health sector a "deep black hole" with regard to how money is used.

"The myriad ways in which funds are spent means that we cannot know how much money has been spent on this or that aspect of the health sector," she said.

Take the example of medical tourism – the practice of senior civil servants and political leaders (and their families) travelling abroad for healthcare.

"Its cost is unknown," Kobusingye said. "While those who work and pay taxes … die for lack of the most basic care, [money is taken from] – the Ministry of Health, various other ministries, parliament and the State House – to meet the costs of travel, medication and upkeep of the select few in foreign hospitals."

The high number of senior figures who have died in foreign countries while seeking medical care has put a spotlight on Uganda's crumbling health infrastructure.

In 2022, Uganda's speaker of parliament, Jacob Oulanyah, died in Seattle. Emmanuel Tumusiime-Mutebile, the governor of the Central Bank died in Nairobi in the same year. In March 2023, Kenneth Kakuru, justice of the Court of Appeal of Uganda, also died in Nairobi, and soon afterwards, Keith Muhakanizi, permanent secretary in the office of the prime minister, died in Milan.

Anybody who proposes that the government should improve the services at home to save on medical tourism is labelled as callous, as happened when the Ugandan diaspora in Seattle

ABOVE: Ugandan President Yoweri Museveni at the opening of a hospital in Kampala in 2008. Censorship and fear have meant that the declining quality of healthcare in Ugandan hospitals goes under the radar

protested against the millions of dollars spent on Oulanyah. The chief justice of Uganda, Alfonse Owiny-Dollo, declared the protesters "wicked".

With such a judgment from the country's top judge, what are the chances that censorship in the health sector can be fought? ✖

Danson Kahyana teaches at Boston College and is a research fellow at the Centre for Gender and Africa Studies, University of Free State, South Africa. He is Index's contributing editor for East Africa

SPECIAL REPORT ◆ THE FORGOTTEN PATIENTS

Left speechless

The psychological toll of living in a warzone is causing children in Gaza to lose their ability to communicate, writes **SARAH DAWOOD**

MOST CHILDREN SAY their first word between the ages of 12 and 18 months. But Fatehy, a Palestinian boy living in Jabalia City in Gaza, is four years old and is still barely talking.

When he does speak, he says the same words over and over again – "scared", "bomb" and "fighters". While he used to say words such as "mumma" and "bubba", his language progression has reversed, and now he is mostly silent.

He has been displaced roughly 15 times and experienced several close family deaths, including those of his mother and sister. At one point, he was discovered on a pile of bodies and was presumed dead. He was rescued purely by luck when a family member saw that he was still gently breathing.

His cousin, Nejam, is three years old. His speech is also very limited, and is mostly reserved for the names of tanks, drones and rockets. He has been pulled from rubble several times.

Neither child has access to school, nursery or social activities with friends. Medical treatment is severely limited, and they have been unable to access any of the few speech therapists available. Food scarcity also means they have been unable to learn basic vocabulary about ingredients or meals.

Dalloul Neder, a 33-year-old

SPECIAL REPORT

LEFT: Children play in the rubble of a destroyed building in Rafah in the southern Gaza Strip, January 2025

Palestinian man living in the UK since 2017, is their uncle.

"The only thing they've been listening to is the bombing," he told Index. "That's why they are traumatised.

"They miss their families, grandparents, mums and family gatherings around the table. They realise something is not right but they can't express their pain."

Psychological trauma is extremely common for children living in warzones. This can cause mental health issues such as depression, anxiety and panic attacks, but also communication problems, such as losing the ability to speak partially or fully, or developing a stammer. For younger children such as Fatehy and Nejam, war trauma can impact cognitive development, causing language delays and making it hard to learn to speak in the first place.

In December, the Gaza-based psychosocial support organisation Community Training Centre for Crisis Management published a report based on interviews it had conducted with more than 500 children, parents and caregivers. Nearly all the children interviewed (96%) said they felt that death was "imminent" and 77% of them avoided talking about traumatic events. Many showed signs of withdrawal and severe anxiety. Roughly half the caregivers said children exhibited signs of introversion, with some reporting that they spent a lot of time alone and did not like to interact with others.

Katrin Glatz Brubakk is a child psychotherapist who has just returned to Norway from Gaza, where she was working as a mental health activities manager with Médecins Sans Frontières in Nasser Hospital, Khan Younis. Her team offers mental health support to adults and children, but mainly to children dealing with burns and orthopaedic injuries, mostly from bomb attacks.

She told Index that children tended to present with "acute trauma responses", while the long-term impacts on their psychological wellbeing were yet to be seen.

In her work, she typically sees two types of responses – either restlessness and being hard to calm down, or becoming uncommunicative and withdrawn. She believes the latter is significantly harder to spot and therefore under-reported.

"We have to take into account that it's easier to detect the acting-out kids, and it's easier to overlook the withdrawn kids or just think they're a bit shy or quiet," she said.

She commonly saw children experiencing extreme panic attacks due to flashbacks, where any small thing – such as a door closing or their parent leaving a room – could trigger them. She noted they would often let out "intense screams".

But some children have become so withdrawn they do not scream or cry at all. Some have even fallen into "resignation syndrome", a reduced state of consciousness where they can stop walking, talking and eating entirely.

Brubakk recalled one "extreme case" of a five-year-old boy who was the victim of a bomb attack and witnessed his father die. He fell completely silent and did not want to see anybody, and also hardly ate.

"When children experience severe or multiple trauma, it's as if the body goes into an overload state," she said. "In order to protect themselves from more negative experiences and stress, they totally withdraw from the world."

Living in a warzone can also mean that children's "neural development totally stops", she said, as they lose the opportunity to play, learn new skills, learn language and understand social rules. "The body and mind use all their energy to protect the child from more harm," she said. "That doesn't affect the child only there and then, it will have long-term consequences."

This is made worse by a lack of "societal structures", such as schools. "[These offer a] social arena, where they can feel success – there's no normality, there's no predictability."

Therapy can be used to encourage children to speak again, particularly with creative methods such as play and →

 The body and mind use all their energy to protect the child from more harm

→ drawing therapy. Brubakk explained how through "playful activities" and "small steps", her team were able to encourage children to communicate.

Recently, she managed this through the creation of a makeshift dolls house. A young girl had been burnt in a bomb attack. Her two brothers had been killed and her two sisters injured, with one of them in a critical state. It was uncertain whether her sister would survive.

The girl wasn't able to speak about her experiences until Brubakk helped her create a dolls house using an old box, some colouring pens and tape, plus two small dolls the girl had kept from her home. She named the dolls after herself and her sister, and was able to start expressing her grief and fears, as well as her hopes for the future.

"So through a very different type of communication, she was able to express how worried she was about her sister, but also process some of the experiences she had," said Brubakk.

A report published by the non-profit Gaza Community Mental Health Programme (GCMHP) includes success stories of children who have benefited from creative communication. Alaa, a 12-year-old boy who sustained facial injuries after a bombardment and then later experienced forced evacuation by Israeli forces from Al-Shifa hospital, developed recurring nightmares, verbal violence, memory loss and an aversion to talking about his injuries. A treatment plan of drawing therapy and written narrations of the events helped him to become more sociable, and now he visits other injured children to share his story with them and listen to theirs.

Sarah, meanwhile, is a 13-year-old girl who developed post-traumatic stress disorder and traumatic mutism after having an operation on her leg following a shell attack. She didn't speak

She didn't speak for three months and would use only signals or write on pieces of paper

for three months and would use only signals or write on pieces of paper. The GCMHP worked with her on a gradual psychotherapy plan, including drawing and play therapy. After three weeks, she started saying a few words, and she was eventually able to start discussing her trauma with therapists.

Trauma-related speech issues are complex problems that can be diagnosed as both mental health issues and communication disorders, so they often benefit from intervention from both psychotherapists and speech and language therapists.

Alongside developing speech issues due to war, living in a warzone can worsen speech problems in children with pre-existing conditions. For example, those with developmental disabilities such as autism may already have selective mutism (talking only in certain settings or circumstances), and this can become more pronounced.

Then there is behaviour that can become "entrenched" due to their environments, Ryann Sowden told Index. Sowden is a UK-based health researcher and speech and language therapist who has previously worked with bilingual children, including refugees who developed selective mutism in warzones.

"Sometimes, [in warzones,] it's not always safe to talk," she said. "One family I worked with had to be quiet to keep safe. So, I can imagine things like that become more entrenched, as it's a way of coping with seeing some really horrific things."

She described a "two-pronged" effect, with war trauma causing or exacerbating speech issues, and a lack of healthcare services meaning that early intervention for those with existing communication disorders or very young children can't happen.

There is an understandable need to focus on survival rather than rehabilitation in warzones, she said, and a lot of allied health professionals, such as occupational therapists, physiotherapists and psychotherapists, are diverted to emergency services.

This was echoed by Julie Marshall, emerita professor of communication disability at Manchester Metropolitan

RIGHT: Children walk amongst debris in Al-Mawasi, Gaza. A lack of normal societal structures such as schools are impacting their development

University and formerly a speech and language therapist working with refugees in Rwanda. Her academic research has noted a lack of speech and language therapists in low and middle-income countries (LMICs) in general.

"In many LMICs, communication professionals are rare, resulting in reliance on community members or a community-based rehabilitation workforce underprepared to work with people with communication disorders," she wrote in a co-authored paper in British Medical Journal Global Health.

For children who already have speech or language difficulties, losing family members who are attuned to their other methods of communication, such as gestures or pointing, can make the issue worse.

"If you are non-verbal, you may well have a family member who understands an awful lot of what we would call 'non-intentional communication'," said Marshall. "If you lose the person who knows you and reads you really well, that's huge."

In warzones, Marshall and Sowden both believe that speech and language therapy is more likely to be incorporated alongside medical disciplines dealing with physical injury, such as head or neck trauma or dysphagia (an inability to swallow correctly). This belief was mirrored by the work of Brubakk, whose mental health team at Nasser Hospital worked mostly with patients who had been seen in the burns and orthopaedics departments.

One of the most valuable things that can be done is to train communities in simple ways to help children who may be living with a speech or language difficulty, Marshall believes, shifting away from treating a single individual to trying to change the general environment.

"There are lots of attitudes around communication disabilities that could be changed," she said. For example, it is often misjudged that children with muteness may not want to talk, and they are subsequently ignored rather than patiently and gently interacted with.

Despite a lack of healthcare provision, there are some professionals on the ground in Gaza. In 2024, the UN interviewed Amina al-Dahdouh, a speech and language therapist working in a tent west of Al-Zawaida. She said that for every 10 children she saw, six suffered from speech problems such as stammering. In a video report, al-Dahdouh held a mirror up to children's faces as she tried to teach them basic Arabic vocabulary and show them how to formulate the sounds in their mouths.

But the destruction of medical facilities such as hospitals and a lack of equipment have made it difficult for professionals to do their jobs. Mohammed el-Hayek is a 36-year-old Palestinian speech and language therapist based in Gaza City who previously worked with Syrian child refugees in Turkey.

"Currently, there are no clinics or centres to treat children, and there are many cases that I cannot treat because of the war, destruction and lack of necessary tools – the most important of which is soundproof rooms," he told Index. "Before the war, I used to treat children in their homes."

Soundproof rooms can be used by speech and language therapists to create more private, quiet and controlled spaces that reduce distracting external noises including triggering sounds such as gunfire or bombs.

The most common issue he has encountered is stammering, which he says becomes harder to tackle the longer it is left untreated.

"Children are never supported in terms of speech and language," he added. "[It is] considered 'not essential' but it is the most important thing so that the child can communicate with all their family and friends and not cause [them] psychological problems."

For many of these children, the road to recovery will be long. Mona el-Farra, a doctor and director of Gaza projects for the Middle East Children's Alliance,

ABOVE: There are few facilities for children in Gaza living with psychological trauma and speech and language difficulties

told Index that the "accumulation of trauma" caused by multiple bombardments meant that even those receiving psychological support were offered little respite to heal.

One glimmer of hope is that cultural barriers around trauma appear to be lifting, which has encouraged people to stop self-censoring around their own mental health.

"There is no stigma now [around mental health]," said el-Farra. "The culture used to be like this, but not anymore. You can see that 99% of the population has been subjected to trauma. [People] have started to express themselves and not deny it."

At the time of publishing, the ceasefire between Israel and Hamas had broken down and bombardment had restarted. When a permanent ceasefire is finally established and healthcare provision in Gaza can be rebuilt, there will need to be a concerted effort to support children with their psychological and social rehabilitation as well as their physical health. Hopefully then they can start to come to terms with their experiences and tell their stories – otherwise, they could be lost forever. ✘

Sarah Dawood is editor at Index on Censorship

SPECIAL REPORT ◆ THE FORGOTTEN PATIENTS

Speaking up to end the cut

Somalia has a widespread female genital mutilation problem, and the activists fighting for women and girls are at risk, writes **HINDA ABDI MOHAMOUD**

"SOMEONE CALLED ME on my local number and threatened me, saying, 'If you don't stop what you're doing, you will be dead'," activist Shamsa Hassan, who did not want to use her real name, told Index.

Female genital mutilation (FGM) remains a deeply entrenched practice in Somalia, with some of the highest prevalence rates in the world. Sometimes known as "cutting" or "female circumcision", the practice is carried out for non-medical reasons and has many harmful impacts.

According to Unicef, approximately 99% of women and girls over the age of 15 in Somalia have undergone some form of FGM, making it one of the countries most affected by this harmful practice. While there has not been a recent rise in reported cases, the practice remains pervasive due to cultural, social and religious factors.

Activists working to end FGM in Somalia demonstrate immense bravery in the face of entrenched cultural and social norms. They confront deeply rooted traditions, stigma and resistance from traditionalists who consider FGM as a requirement. These activists often face direct threats including violence, harassment and public shaming.

Hassan explained: "I have been

an activist since 2016, but the unsafe environment in the country makes it difficult to openly discuss issues. When people see someone advocating for a cause or FGM, they often say, 'This person is brainwashed, believes in something different', and attack you."

She said she avoided public spaces as she still got harassed, and she was worried about people sharing her personal information with those who could harm or threaten her.

Ifrah Ahmed is the founder and director of the Ifrah Foundation, which she established in 2010. The organisation has a goal to end FGM in Somalia, and Ahmed – who is Somali-Irish – has dedicated her time to addressing this issue.

"When I returned to the country from abroad, it was not easy to openly discuss FGM or harassment-related issues," she told Index. "Many people accused me of being influenced by Western culture, saying things like, 'You've been brainwashed; go back to where you came from'. Others claimed that my efforts were solely motivated by financial gain, saying, 'You just want to make money out of this'."

She launched the Dear Daughter campaign to raise awareness of FGM and combat the practice. Through it, she asked communities, families, religious leaders and midwives to commit to not cutting their daughters.

However, this work comes with significant challenges.

"I often face threats and insults on social media," she said. "Some people accuse me of opposing religion, trying to change our culture or working on behalf of foreign interests."

Asad Abukar, a human rights defender and FGM activist, told Index: "For the past 10 years, I have been working on human rights, gender-based violence and FGM issues in Somalia. As an FGM activist, I have faced numerous challenges from society. People often shame me, saying, 'How can you, as a man, talk about FGM and women's issues?' Others question me, asking, 'Don't you have anything else to do?'"

According to Abukar, human rights activists face constant threats, from phone calls and direct confrontations to emails and social media messages.

He once received an email saying: "We know what your organisation does and the work you're involved in. You need to stop what you're doing."

"Last year, I received a particularly serious threat over the phone that posed a significant danger to my life," he said. "This incident forced me to change all my contact information and daily routines. Previously I would answer

Many people accused me of being influenced by Western culture

calls from unknown numbers, but due to the threats I no longer respond to them. The goal of these threats is to instill fear and discourage us from continuing our work."

Abukar admits there are times he considers leaving the country, and that many of his colleagues have already done so because of the threats they've received.

Fatima Ismail has been an activist for about nine years, raising awareness about FGM. She has written a book examining the different types of FGM and their associated health complications.

"If you are an FGM activist, people often question you, asking, 'Are you a survivor of FGM? Why are you talking about this issue?'" she said.

"When I first began activism, I started with a research study. I wanted to learn more about the different types of FGM so I visited one of the camps in Mogadishu. However, when I arrived, the people there didn't understand my intentions and accused me of trying to kidnap their children. They stoned me and I had to run away to protect myself."

Ultimately, she told Index, many people want her and other activists to stop their work. But despite the threats, they will not stop talking about FGM and fighting for the women and girls who are left traumatised by the practice. ✖

Hinda Abdi Mohamoud is the chief editor of Bilan, Somalia's first all-women media house in Mogadishu. Funded by the European Union through UNDP and hosted by Dalsan Media Group, Bilan shines a light on the issues women care about and offers a platform for women's voices

LEFT: A group of Somali women discussing the dangers of female genital mutilation (FGM) in Baidoa, Somalia

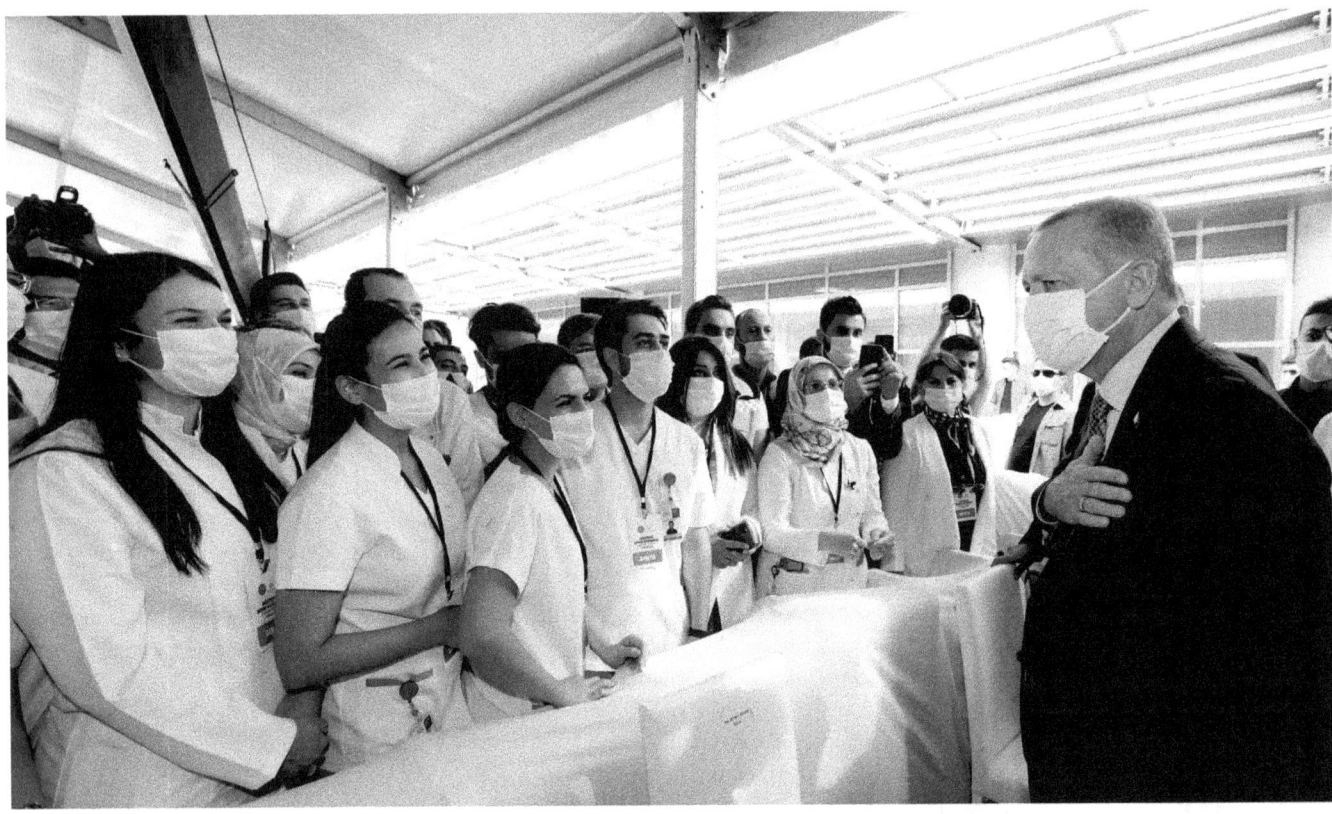

SPECIAL REPORT ◆ THE FORGOTTEN PATIENTS

Doctors under attack

Whilst president Recep Tayyip Erdoğan claims Turkey's healthcare is flourishing, medics are paying the price for speaking out against false government claims or discriminatory policies, writes **KAYA GENÇ**

SINCE HIS JUSTICE and Development Party (AKP) ascended to power in 2002, Recep Tayyip Erdoğan has boasted about Turkey's healthcare. Under his watch, the AKP introduced its Health Transformation Programme in 2003 – a flurry of reforms that aimed to improve the efficiency, quality and accessibility of health services.

The World Bank applauded these changes, concluding that "Turkey significantly improved the supply of services" between 2003 and 2013. Set up on a combination of national and private health insurance, the country's healthcare is also affordable, with all residents and citizens able to access services for a small monthly premium the equivalent of about $20.

The success of the healthcare system meant it soon became a political tool in the hands of an increasingly authoritarian government. In election campaigns over the past decade, Erdoğan frequently showed footage of hospital queues from the 1990s. He boasted of having revived a healthcare system that, he warned, would collapse if the opposition ended his reign.

But for Turkey's health professionals there is a different side to the story – medics complain of being overworked, underpaid and regularly subjected to abuse.

Roughly 88% of Turkey's medics (100,000) are members of the Turkish Medical Association (TTB), which has branches in 54 provinces. The professional body and registered trade union monitors medical practitioners' grievances and issues reports annually. For this reason, the government has continually attacked the TTB.

As medics dealt with the Covid-19 pandemic in September 2020, Devlet Bahçeli – whose Nationalist Movement Party (MHP) governs in a coalition with the AKP – called for the TTB to be

SPECIAL REPORT

OPPOSITE: Turkish President Erdoğan has bragged of the improvements his government made to healthcare – but health professionals tell a different story

shut down and for its leadership to be prosecuted. In 2023, an Istanbul court sentenced the union's leader, Şebnem Korur Fincancı, to nearly three years in jail on charges of disseminating "terror organisation propaganda" – a move seen by human rights groups as an attempt to silence government criticism.

Even before the tenure of Fincancı, who is a highly-regarded human rights defender, TTB members have found themselves in trouble with the authorities.

In 2018, TTB's central council warned that the violent clashes between Kurdish militants and Turkish security forces threatened public health. The union released a statement titled "War is a public health problem", and Erdoğan subsequently made a speech calling the TTB "terrorist lovers" and deriding its anti-war rhetoric. He went on to investigate TTB members who had signed the statement and dismiss them from roles in the Ministry of Health.

In an interview with Index, Alpay Azap, who was elected TTB's president in June 2024, said little had changed regarding the strife between his organisation and the government. "Whether people can freely speak their minds and point out shortcomings is a health issue," he said. "Freedom of expression is essential to protect public health."

Azap complained that warnings issued by TTB continued to be ignored due to "political considerations" and fears 2025 will be an even more challenging year.

One development that has caused concern is Erdoğan's declaration that 2025 will be the Year of the Family.

RIGHT: Members of the Turkish Medical Association (TTB) and other health professionals protest in Ankara against Erdoğan and the silencing of health workers

Claiming that population growth was essential for the nation's "survival", the president laid out a series of policies in January aimed to support traditional family values, such as financial support for young couples, in a bid to reverse Turkey's declining fertility rate. While some of these measures appear to offer benefits to some citizens, they marginalise others, with Erdoğan even referring to LGBTQ+ people as a "poison injected into the family institution".

For Azap, this was also a clarion call for doctor bashing. "After this speech, if we make a statement as medics about protecting female health [through] family planning then the government will target us," he said. "But we protect female health nevertheless. The government may have an agenda of its own and consider, for example, Turkey's ageing population as a problem. But risking young women's health to grow birth rates is unacceptable."

There has also been intimidation of TTB members and other medical professionals who have raised concerns with the government or challenged its narrative, as seen during the pandemic.

"There were multiple court cases against our medics who published scientific data, especially during Covid-19," Azap said. According to the TTB, the government threatened

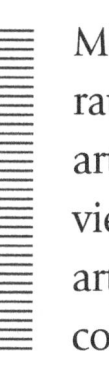

Medics would rather not articulate their views at all than articulate them covertly

doctors who posted online about local virus outbreaks with criminal charges in an attempt to hide the extent of the pandemic's spread.

Many doctors were threatened with prosecution. Among these were Özgür Deniz Değer, co-chair of the TTB's branch in the eastern city of Van, who was charged for "creating fear and panic among the people". The charges, which were later dropped, came after he posted on X (formerly Twitter) that he was uncertain about the government's health worker pandemic death toll.

Kayıhan Pala, a professor of public health, also faced a disciplinary investigation for sharing his views on the numbers of reported cases in Bursa, and for accusing the government of understating cases and deaths.

Despite the risks, Azap says →

CREDIT: (Erdoğan) Xinhua / Alamy; (protest) Tunahan Turhan / SOPA Images / Sipa USA

ABOVE: Murals in Ankara dedicated to medical workers in Turkey, created in solidarity with protests by the Turkish Medical Association (TTB)

→ anonymity isn't a tactic used by doctors when publishing sensitive data. "Medics would rather not articulate their views at all than articulate them covertly," he said. "Most medics deal with economic difficulties, and I understand they can't always speak out."

The conflict between the union and the government is also due to workers' rights issues. TTB has supported strike action over the past year, with family doctors staging walkouts for 13 days between October 2024 and January 2025 over untenable working conditions, requirements to see between 80 and 100 patients a day, and substandard medical centres.

The government is largely in control of the media narrative surrounding doctors, said Azap.

"This is the big problem in Turkey's healthcare world: the lack of a free press, which allows the government to say what they like to the masses. Social media is the only means to make our voice heard," he said.

Attacks in the media have sometimes led to violence. Psychiatrist Koray Başar is among those who have been physically attacked for their professional activities. Başar, a faculty member at the department of psychiatry at Hacettepe University, has received backlash for his work in the field of gender-affirming surgery.

In November 2021, the right-wing, government-aligned newspaper Milat published an article on Başar headlined "Stop the LGBT missionary doctor!".

The article claimed Başar was "carrying out scandalous LGBT activities at Hacettepe University Hospital where he works".

It said he was "organising conferences for trans women at the same hospital" and participating "in LGBT's so-called pride marches".

Seven months after the article was published, Başar was attacked outside his home by two people. They beat him and demanded that he stop his work and LGBTQ+ advocacy.

A month later, a protest was staged by unions and healthcare professionals in solidarity with Başar outside the TTB's building.

Başar told Index he had stopped expressing his views online since the attack. "I used to use Twitter and Instagram. Now, even if I share a picture of a flower, I receive threats," he said. "Since my attack I can't use social media. I also noticed how colleagues who haven't been targeted like me refrain from using these platforms out of fear."

The discourse in Turkey "emboldens violent acts and makes life very hard for anyone who opposes discrimination", he said. "It now takes real courage to speak out."

Access to gender-affirming surgeries has become increasingly challenging, exacerbated by the fact that doctors offering such procedures are becoming more and more stigmatised. "Even compared with the pre-pandemic era, the situation is worse today," Başar said. "There have always been problems accessing sex-related health services as it is tough to reach psychiatrists who work in the field."

Since being attacked in the media, Başar lost his visibility in the medical world. Before the pandemic, he would get invitations to talk about gender-affirming surgeries and hormone therapy – he no longer receives such invitations. He has also noticed that academics who used to write reports on gender affirmation procedures are now more reluctant to do so.

He fears that Erdoğan's disingenuous so-called Year of the Family could bring more hostility towards LGBTQ+ communities and also worries that Turkey could move in the direction of Russia and Georgia, by banning gender-affirming surgeries altogether.

The rise in hostility towards marginalised groups is directly related to the strength of the networks available to support them, Başar believes. Because medical unions such as the TTB are increasingly ostracised, it means their members are less able to advocate for patients.

"What keeps people strong when they're under discriminatory assault is this network of solidarity that protects them," he said. "In Turkey, those networks themselves are under assault."

Whilst Erdoğan sings the praises of Turkey's healthcare system, the impact of his government's negative attitude towards medical professionals could ultimately mean the country suffers. The risks that doctors face when they speak the truth, publicly support minority groups or publish forward-thinking academic papers means that many young people may now "think twice before applying for medical schools", said Başar. ✖

Kaya Genç is a contributing editor for Index on Censorship based in Istanbul

54(01):66/68|DOI:10.1177/03064220251332631

> I used to use Twitter and Instagram. Now, even if I share a picture of a flower, I receive threats

CREDIT: ruellervelle / Alamy

SPECIAL REPORT ✦ THE FORGOTTEN PATIENTS

Denial of healthcare is censoring political prisoners – often permanently

Three writers from India, Russia and Uganda share shocking stories of dissidents who have been refused access to medical treatment in prison

IT SEEMS OBVIOUS to say that being in prison is bad for your health but the research is damning. In the UK, for example, prisoners use healthcare services three times more frequently than the general population and have poorer health outcomes.

While poor prisoner health has many causes, in authoritarian regimes denying access to healthcare is actively weaponised to persecute prisoners, such as Chinese human rights activist Guo Feixiong and Iranian Nobel Prize winner Narges Mohammadi. In some cases, this denial of healthcare has arguably led to the prisoners' deaths: Vladimir Putin critic Alexei Navalny and the Belarusian artist Ales Pushkin both died in jail after not receiving essential or adequate treatment.

Index contributors Rishabh Jain, Alexandra Domenech and Danson Kahyana share stories of political prisoners around the world who have been denied vital healthcare.

54(01):69/71|DOI:10.1177/03064220251332632

The tragic case of GN Saibaba: A life crushed by neglect in prison

By RISHABH JAIN

GOKARAKONDA NAGA (GN) Saibaba, a professor of English at Delhi University – an Indian university known for its academic excellence – was arrested in May 2014 under the Unlawful Activities (Prevention) Act. This anti-terrorism law, often criticised for its broad and vague provisions, allows authorities to detain people accused of activities deemed a threat to national security without requiring substantial evidence. Saibaba, who contracted polio at the age of five and was disabled due to post-polio paralysis, was accused of being associated with the banned Communist Party of India (Maoist) and of advocating for the rights of marginalised tribal communities in conflict-ridden regions.

Despite his disability and pre-existing medical conditions, Saibaba was incarcerated in the Nagpur Central Jail under harsh conditions that exacerbated his fragile health. His confinement in an anda (egg-shaped) cell, devoid of natural light and ventilation, marked the beginning of a rapid physical decline. Saibaba's health issues – diabetes, hypertension and a paralytic condition in his left arm caused by an injury during his arrest – were poorly managed in prison. Denied access to an assistant to help with basic activities such as brushing his teeth or using the toilet, he often relied on inconsistent help from fellow inmates, leaving him in a state of indignity and helplessness.

During his time in prison, Saibaba contracted swine flu, which further weakened his immune system. In August 2022, he developed severe, continuous fevers, making him susceptible to Covid-19. The virus left him with persistent cold symptoms, blackouts and worsening paralysis, yet medical care remained inadequate. While prison doctors recommended his transfer to hospital, no action was taken.

Psychological trauma compounded his suffering. In 2020, he was denied permission to attend his mother's funeral, even via video call. Saibaba was released in March 2024 after a decade of incarceration, but his body had suffered irreparable damage. He died in October 2024, a victim of systemic neglect. His case highlights how prison conditions in India are used to silence activists.

Rishabh Jain is a freelance journalist based in New Delhi, India

ABOVE: GN Saibaba contracted polio at the age of five and was accused of advocating for the rights of marginalised tribal communities in conflict-ridden regions

CREDIT: Muzammil Sidheeqi / CC BY-SA 4.0

Russian prisons: just what the doctor wouldn't order

By ALEXANDRA DOMENECH

ABOVE: Natalya Filonova was not treated for her heart condition, diabetes or hypertension while in prison in Russia

NOW 63, NATALYA Filonova started her activism in the 1990s and published the only independent newspaper in the Russian city of Petrovsk-Zabaykalsky.

In April 2022, she spent five days in jail for demanding a bus driver take off the "Z" – the symbol of Vladimir Putin's war in Ukraine – displayed on a vehicle.

In September, Filonova went out to protest against the military draft. She was arrested and accused of "violence" against the police – for allegedly hitting an officer, stabbing another with a pen and breaking a finger of yet another officer. Almost a year later, she was sentenced to two years and 10 months in a penal colony.

While on trial, Filonova was placed under house arrest, during which time her husband had a heart attack. Her 16-year-old adopted disabled son was staying with him at that time. She went to see them – and, despite having informed the authorities of the situation, she was thrown in detention for breaking her house arrest order.

While she was in custody, her son was sent to an orphanage and her relatives were not allowed to take care of him. He was subjected to harassment and violence there – which, he claimed, was organised by the orphanage's administration.

Filonova has a heart condition, diabetes and hypertension. She wasn't prescribed treatment for these health issues in the detention centre and was given unknown medication instead. Also, she wasn't informed of the results of a cancer screening she underwent. And in April 2024, when she had a high fever, the authorities refused to call a doctor.

> **Filonova wasn't prescribed treatment for her health issues in the detention centre**

Despite the pressure, in May 2024, in a letter sent from the colony where she had been transferred, she wrote that she had turned down an offer of amnesty because she refused to plead guilty.

Following her refusal to co-operate, Filonova was put in a punishment cell on three occasions. On top of this, she was detained under "strict detention conditions", with restrictions including being allowed out to walk for only an hour and a half a day. These methods, which can lead to serious health implications, are commonly used by the Russian authorities against their imprisoned opponents.

Alexandra Domenech is a Moscow-born, Paris-based journalist specialising in women's rights in Russia

SPECIAL REPORT

Activist's poetry stands testament to healthcare denial in Uganda

By **DANSON KAHYANA**

WHEN STELLA NYANZI, a Ugandan academic, activist and writer, was imprisoned in Luzira Women's Prison in Kampala for 475 days from 2018 until 2020 for speaking truth to power, she clandestinely wrote poetry to document her incarcerated life.

Released in 2020 a few days before she gained her freedom, her poetry collection No Roses From My Mouth documents several health issues that incarcerated women face in prison.

The opening poem, A Plea for Decongestion, depicts the women inmates as "sleep[ing] as congested as firewood neatly stacked", some on bare concrete because they lack bedding, leading to diseases such as pneumonia.

In Kitintale Fills Up Again, Nyanzi vividly captures the sanitation deficiencies of the women's prison where more than 600 inmates are served by just two pit latrines which fill up and overflow regularly, forcing women to improvise "on papers tossed behind wards", "in menstrual hygiene pails" and "in prison rags for mopping". One can imagine the health implications of this kind of environment, including mental health issues – especially for those inmates who are forced to clean the overflowing mess.

In No Medicine Again, she captures the agony that inmates experience because of the myriad diseases they pick up from the dirty prison. "We scratch our detained dark vulvas / vulvas itching sweeter than anuses with pinworms", she writes, painting a grim picture of a place infested with urinary tract infections.

Other diseases she records include fevers, diabetes, high blood pressure, arthritis and "wretched coughs" that echo through prison walls, "dry coughs that burn like new fires /

> Nyanzi writes of "babies miscarried from wombs of prisoners"

wet coughs drawing smelly yellow catarrh". These diseases mostly go untreated.

In Babies in Prison, Nyanzi writes about "babies miscarried from wombs of prisoners / as wardresses mock and jeer".

The autobiographical poem, I Miscarried Justice, details a miscarriage the poet suffered. When she starts bleeding, rather than take her to a proper medical facility, the prison officers allegedly beat her and declare her a liar who could not possibly suffer a miscarriage because she is postmenopausal. Even when she twice slides into a coma, the officers remain aloof.

Now exiled in Germany, Nyanzi is contemplating suing the Ugandan prison service to get justice for her miscarried baby.

Danson Kahyana *teaches at Boston College and is a research fellow at the University of Free State, South Africa*

BELOW: Stella Nyanzi's poetry documents the appalling state of Uganda's prisons

SPECIAL REPORT ♦ THE FORGOTTEN PATIENTS

The silent killer

MACKENZIE ARGENT speaks to author and doctor **ANNABEL SOWEMIMO** about the difficulties of speaking out against institutional racism in the UK's National Health Service

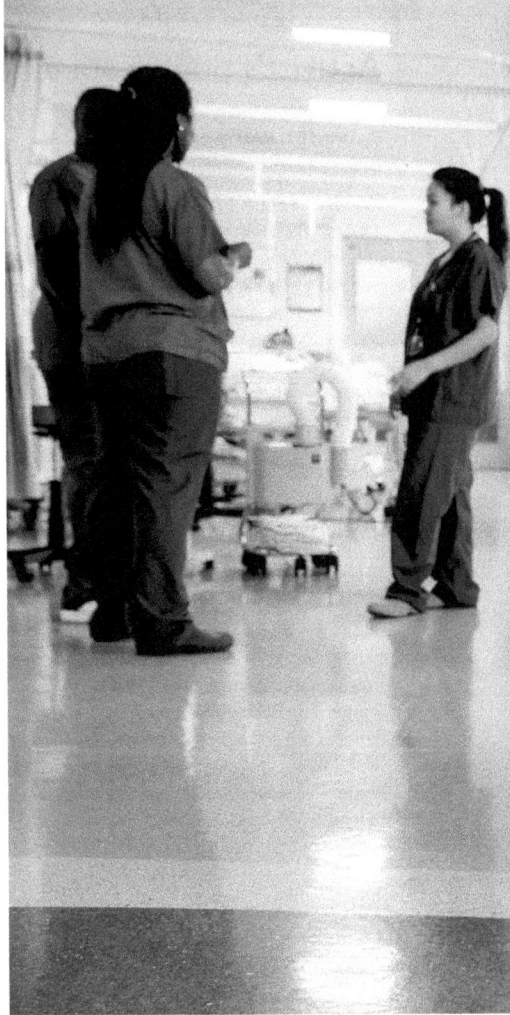

FOR THOSE REGULARLY subjected to racial discrimination, it can be exhausting to encourage people without this firsthand experience to see things from their perspective. Convincing others that certain behaviours or attitudes are harmful can be frustrating, difficult and ultimately lead to hostility – and nowhere more so than within large organisations, where prejudice may be deeply embedded.

The National Health Service (NHS) is one of the UK's most loved and largest institutions, employing more people than any other organisation in the country. But, as a result, it is not exempt from societal issues.

Institutional racism within the NHS, impacting both staff and patients, has been well documented. A report compiled last year by Middlesex University and the charity Brap found that "racial prejudice remains embedded in the health service despite initiatives to remove it".

The NHS has failed to "provide a safe and effective means for listening to and dealing with concerns" raised by Black and minority ethnic (BME) staff, and it noted a "culture of avoidance, defensiveness or minimisation of the issue from their employer if they did so".

Nearly three-quarters of UK-trained staff had complained of race discrimination, according to the study.

A survey commissioned by the membership body NHS Confederation in 2022 also reported that more than half of its surveyed BME NHS leaders had considered leaving in the three years beforehand as a result of racist treatment they had experienced while doing their jobs.

Black patients also often find their concerns ignored by healthcare professionals, with potentially deadly consequences.

Dr Annabel Sowemimo, a doctor of sexual and reproductive health and author of the book Divided: Racism, Medicine and Why We Need to Decolonise Healthcare, has spent many years facing and exploring this prejudice, and has seen her own concerns ignored as both a patient and a practitioner.

Speaking to Index, she told a story from her time as a junior doctor working in the paediatric accident and emergency department, when a Somali child came in experiencing abdominal pain but with "atypical symptoms".

An experienced nurse said the child needed to go home with antibiotics, as they had a urinary tract infection. But Sowemimo was not convinced by this diagnosis.

"I saw the patient and I said, 'I don't really think that this child has an UTI'," she said. "The dad didn't really speak great English so it was difficult to communicate."

Ultimately, the child was diagnosed with severe appendicitis and needed surgery. "If they had not had surgery [the appendix] probably would have ruptured – that's what the surgeon said to me," Sowemimo added.

"It was really hard, because I was a really junior doctor, I had been in the department for only a few weeks, and the nurse was quite senior and I didn't want to be seen to be going against what she said."

Sowemimo, who is from a Nigerian background, believes that a combination of cultural bias from staff and culturally influenced self-censorship by patients can play a collective role in misdiagnoses.

"I don't think that nurse was being

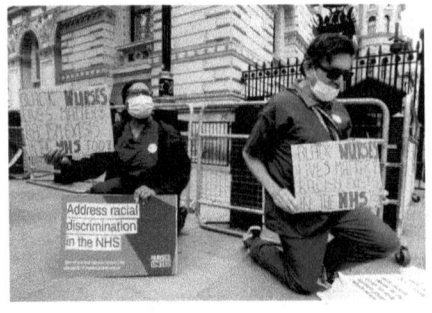

ABOVE: NHS workers demonstrate in aid of better pay and the Black Lives Matter movement at the gates of Downing Street in June 2020

SPECIAL REPORT

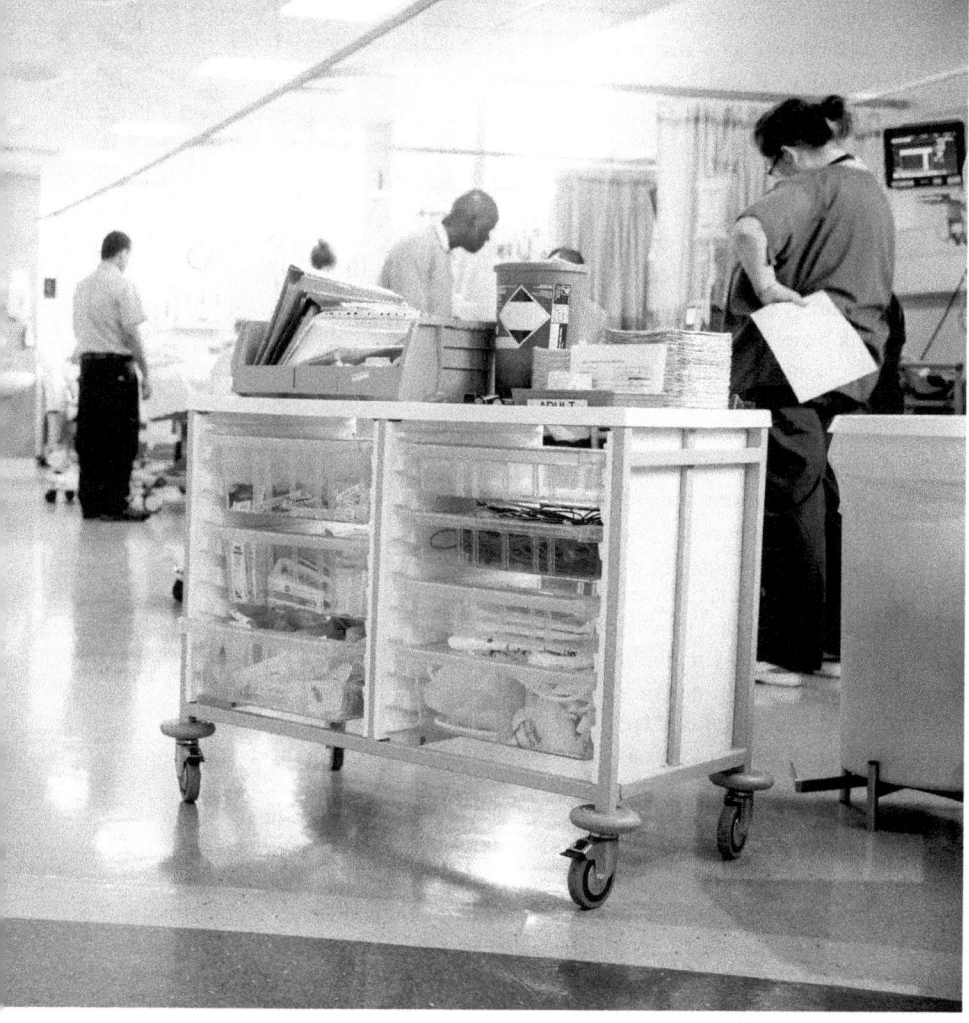

LEFT: A recent survey found that nearly three quarters of UK-trained NHS staff had complained of race discrimination

A misguided belief that Black women "exaggerate" their symptoms has also proven to be fatal, and nowhere more so than in maternity care. Black women in the UK are nearly four times more likely to die in pregnancy and childbirth than their white counterparts.

In 2023, an investigation into the death of a pregnant Black woman in Liverpool found "cultural and ethnic bias" played a part in her late diagnosis and death. Hospital staff had neglected to take some observations because she was "being difficult", according to comments in her medical notes. This delayed her diagnosis and treatment and led to her baby dying, and then to her own death two days later.

Such biases are endemic in many countries, and ethnic minorities faced higher mortality rates during the pandemic.

Black American doctor Susan Moore documented on social media how her pain and requests for medicine were ignored when she was in hospital with Covid-19 in 2020. She said she was made to feel like a "drug addict" for requesting remdesivir, the antiviral drug used to treat Covid patients. She later died due to complications from the virus.

In May 2020, the British Medical Association (BMA) reported that more than 90% of all doctors and consultants who had lost their lives from Covid-19 up until that point had been from minority ethnic backgrounds. →

racist, but there were certain things that made this child more vulnerable," she said. "Culturally, I think the child had probably been raised in an environment like mine.

"I would, as a kid, never make a scene in public because my Nigerian parents just wouldn't stand for that kind of thing. So sometimes, if I was uncomfortable, even around adults, I'd just hold that energy in, whereas other children could probably express that more."

Sowemimo believes that self-silencing can be particularly pervasive among Black patients, who may have fears around their expressions of pain or discomfort being construed as "aggression" by healthcare professionals.

"We change our behaviour," she said. "We're worried about being seen as 'angry, Black women' in particular. So even if I am in pain, I'm not going to feel comfortable yelling and writhing around. It doesn't mean that I'm [less] in pain [than] the next person, just that I'm acutely aware that sometimes things get misread."

 We change our behaviour. We're worried about being seen as "angry, Black women" in particular. So even if I am in pain, I'm not going to feel comfortable yelling and writhing around

→ Sowemimo believes that "biology" is weaponised in healthcare settings, with doctors and nurses often concluding that Black people are more likely to die from certain illnesses due to genetics. There are many complex factors that play into higher death rates, she said, including later diagnoses and a lack of clinical research.

"With some reproductive cancers or endometrial cancer, it seems that Black people present later, and with prostate cancer we have worse outcomes," she said. "We're trying to direct research towards these issues to actually work out what is going on, but ultimately [research isn't funded] towards groups that are not seen as politically mobile, who are more disenfranchised and impoverished.

"Often, people keep telling you that it's biological, that we're all biologically flawed in some way, and this is making us more predisposed to all these things. I think that's actually even more sinister – how people keep on pathologising Blackness rather than addressing the systemic problems that exist."

Beyond the treatment of individuals, systemic issues around resource allocation "compound" the discrimination facing minority groups, she says.

In what think-tank The King's Fund refers to as the "inverse care law", those who most need medical care are least likely to receive it. For example, people who live in the most deprived areas of England are twice as likely to wait more than a year for non-urgent treatment, and there are fewer GPs per patient in more deprived areas. BME people are over-represented in the most deprived areas, and are two to three times more likely to be living in persistent poverty.

Disparities in care are caused by complex societal problems that reach far beyond the realms of healthcare services alone. So changing the behaviour of NHS staff is only the first hurdle, and a high one at that.

"I make this argument a lot in my work, that it's really hard to change something that has been embedded for such a long time," said Sowemimo. "And I think a key part of why we have a lot of these issues [is that] people are just not willing to change their practice."

Broaching inappropriate behaviour can be difficult, given that most NHS staff have good intentions and want to help people. "People… feel like they're underpaid, and they do work particularly altruistically," Sowemimo said. "So telling them that they're not being altruistic, that they might be being biased or discriminatory, people are going to [think that's] quite rude."

In recent years, there has been increasing political scepticism from the government surrounding the need to address inequalities in the NHS. In 2023, for example, the then health secretary Steve Barclay ordered the NHS to stop recruiting for roles by focusing on diversity and inclusion. Health equity commitments have also been discarded – the Maternity Disparities Taskforce set up under former Prime Minister Boris Johnson in 2022 met only twice in 2023 rather than the scheduled six times, and reported little progress.

But there is hope on the horizon: the current Labour government has committed to a Race Equality Act, which includes several provisions around improving healthcare outcomes for BME people, including closing maternal health

ABOVE: A healthcare worker joins a Black Lives Matter march to Parliament Square in July 2020

gaps and improving diversity in clinical trial recruitment.

However, the current geopolitical climate could reverse efforts. US president Donald Trump's executive order banning diversity, equity and inclusion (DEI) programmes across the federal government may have a ripple effect for UK organisations, from which the public sector may not be exempt. "There's a lot of momentum around the push-back; we're very much influenced by US politics," Sowemimo said.

Despite the hurdles, she isn't going to stop banging the drum about healthcare inequalities. "I've always said that, sometimes, the work we're doing is just to stand still," she said. "It's really hard when you're in a time where you're not actually fighting for progress, and no one's going to say, 'You're the person that got that bill [or] that got these people their rights'. In fact, you just fought to make sure their rights weren't removed." ✖

Mackenzie Argent is editorial assistant at Index on Censorship

54(01):72/74|DOI:10.1177/03064220251332633

CREDIT: Andrea Domeniconi / Alamy

I think that's actually even more sinister – how people keep on pathologising Blackness rather than addressing the systemic problems that exist

SPECIAL REPORT ✦ THE FORGOTTEN PATIENTS

Czechoslovakia's haunting legacy

Under Soviet rule, Roma women were subjected to forced sterilisation. **KATIE DANCEY-DOWNS** investigates its insidious impact on the modern-day Czech Republic and Slovakia

ABOVE: A group of Roma women protest in September 2020 for the compensation of women who were unlawfully sterilised

JANA HUSÁROVÁ WAS in labour with her second child when the doctor presented her with a document. "I didn't want to sign it," she said. So she didn't.

"When I got home, I visited my doctor in Sabinov. He told me that my [fallopian tubes] were tied."

She went back to the hospital and asked how that could be possible when she had not signed a consent form.

It was 1984, and Husárová was 15 years old. She is one of many Roma women who have undergone forced sterilisation, as she described in a video for the Slovakian Centre for Civil and Human Rights (known as Poradňa).

Since then, she has fought for justice and compensation, and to stop this happening to other women.

In Soviet-era Czechoslovakia, Roma women underwent forced sterilisations, just as they had done under the Nazi regime.

They were offered money by visiting social workers, pressured into agreeing to the procedure and told that their other children would be taken away if they did not comply. Others were made to sign consent forms while in agony during childbirth, often with no idea what they were signing. When a caesarean section was performed, they were sterilised at the same time.

Then came the Velvet Revolution in 1989 – which marked the end of Soviet rule in Czechoslovakia – and, in 1993, the creation of the Czech Republic and Slovakia as sovereign nations.

Sterilisation was no longer state policy, but the doctors who had implemented it were never punished, and racism towards Roma communities continued to thrive.

And for Roma women, the practice was far from over.

In 2003, a grim reality was uncovered in a report by the global human rights organisation Centre for Reproductive Rights and Poradňa. The organisations interviewed about 110 Roma women across eastern Slovakia who had been (or had likely been) sterilised since the fall of communism. They found that doctors and nurses gave women "misleading or threatening information" to "coerce them into providing last-minute authorisations for sterilisations" when they were undergoing caesareans. C-sections were sometimes given unnecessarily, partly as a pretext for sterilisation.

In some cases, women were not told about the procedure until after the event – if ever.

Alongside forced sterilisation, Roma women faced physical and verbal abuse by medical providers. They were segregated in maternity wards and sent to Roma-only rooms. If they complained, they were insulted by doctors and nurses.

During the course of the research, hospital authorities stopped Roma women accessing their own medical records, denying them the opportunity →

> The fight for Roma women has roots that go back decades

ABOVE: A woman protests outside Ostrava Municipal Hospital. Her sign reads: "Their body – their right". Roma women have been fighting for their rights in the Czech Republic for decades

→ to get to the truth. The government failed to condemn any of these practices or put an end to them. The report writers urged the government to examine the issues and make things right with the survivors.

In 2004, Slovakia adopted new legislation around informed consent, requiring women to wait 30 days before sterilisation could be performed. It also gave more protection to patients seeking access to their medical records.

Soon after the report was published, lawyer Vanda Durbáková started working with Poradňa on a plan to bring some of the cases to court while urging the government to introduce a compensation scheme.

At the time, Slovakia was scheduled to become a member of the European Union (EU), and all eyes were on the state of human rights in the country. The reaction to the report from the state was not welcoming, and it initiated criminal proceedings against the report's authors.

But a group of Roma women felt empowered to take their stories to Parliament.

"They not only submitted their cases in the courts but were also really active, communicating with the media and starting as a group to fight for justice," Durbáková said.

With little luck in the Slovakian courts, they took their cases to the European Court of Human Rights (ECtHR) in Strasbourg.

Between 2011 and 2013, the ECtHR made rulings in three cases, finding that Roma women who had been forcibly sterilised had had their rights violated. The women were granted financial compensation, and the Slovak courts began to make their own rulings in favour of other women, but it was a slow process.

"The women were not really encouraged to take their cases to the courts, because the [Roma] community was afraid of any victimisation," Durbáková said, explaining that they were worried that suing hospitals would lead to further discrimination.

But the women who spoke up told her they believed their actions eventually led to them, and their daughters, getting better treatment.

Roma activist Veronika Cibriková, who was forcibly sterilised in 2000 during a caesarean section, told Poradňa: "I don't want other women – and my daughter, who is now pregnant – to end up like I did. We fight for each and every woman so that they do not suffer as we have suffered." She eventually got justice at the ECtHR.

Following a call for an inquiry by the UN Human Rights Committee, the Slovak government finally apologised in 2021. It promised to pass legislation to allow for financial compensation, but this has not yet come to fruition.

In 2017, CRR and Poradňa published another damning report, documenting Roma women's experiences of

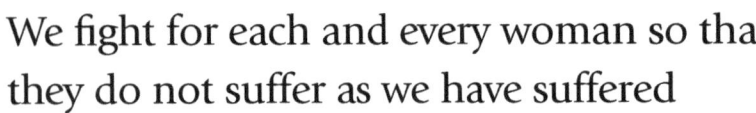

We fight for each and every woman so that they do not suffer as we have suffered

reproductive healthcare in Slovakia. Women reported abuse, discrimination and physical restraint in childbirth. Almost all the women interviewed reported being segregated in maternity units – something the Commissioner for Human Rights condemned during a visit in February 2025.

One woman, Viola, said: "When I was giving birth…they were yelling at women during childbirth… They tied some women's legs or jumped on their bellies. One woman [jumped on my belly] with all her weight, pressed it and yelled, 'Push, push! You were fucking and so now you have to deliver'."

Durbáková said that sometimes Roma-only rooms were so overcrowded that the women had to share beds. Poradňa is now litigating a case against one state-run hospital.

The fight for Roma women has roots that go back decades. The first documentation came in 1978 through the campaigning organisation Charter 77, with signatories including dissident writer (and, later, Czech president) Václav Havel.

It outlined how Roma women were not truly consenting to sterilisation, saying: "Czechoslovak institutions will soon have to answer charges that they are committing genocide."

The Czech Republic is facing this ugly truth, too.

"During the 1990s, we began to hear stories of [Roma] women claiming that they were still being forcibly sterilised," said Gwendolyn Albert, a human rights activist and journalist from the USA who now lives in the Czech Republic. Albert has campaigned for Roma women who have allegedly been sterilised as recently as 2017.

The woman she's worked with the longest is Elena Gorolová, who became the face of the movement to seek justice in the Czech Republic.

Many Roma women felt ashamed that the decision to choose to have a family had been taken away from them, said Albert: "[These women] went to

> [These women] went to the hospital fully believing that the doctors had their best interests at heart and were going to do what was best for their health and what was best for their children

the hospital fully believing that the doctors had their best interests at heart and were going to do what was best for their health and what was best for their children. And instead, they've been tricked into becoming infertile, and so they feel stupid."

Kumar Vishwanathan is the director of Life Together, an NGO working with Roma communities in Ostrava in the Czech Republic. When he found out that he knew many of the women impacted, he brought them together in his office. At first they were tentative to talk but they soon started opening up.

"They were suppressing it within themselves all their lives," he said, adding that some women had faced physical abuse at home after it transpired they could no longer have children. "So that is a taboo which was broken around that table in 2003."

In 2005, the Czech ombudsman published a report showing that there was significant reason to believe that forced sterilisations had continued until at least 2001.

Vishwanathan said that while there was a lot of support for the women during debates in Parliament's Lower House, the problem came in the Upper House.

"A lot of them were doctors, former doctors, who felt threatened that if they agreed to the fact that these women were forcibly sterilised and have to be compensated… they will be challenged as people who violated the law," he said.

The Czech government apologised in 2009, becoming the first in the region to do so. In 2021, Gorolová and others won the fight for women to receive compensation, although the government set a time limit for making a claim. Women had until the end of 2024 to apply, and they had to prove that they had been forcibly sterilised, even though many medical records had allegedly been destroyed or falsified.

The government is now debating a two-year extension of the process, and there are calls to remove the "burden of proof" from the victims and place it on the state instead. However, many women had already been rejected under the earlier rules, had not applied in the first place, or died before they had the chance to seek compensation.

There is likely more yet to be uncovered. Vishwanathan said that many Roma people have told him they still face segregation in Czech hospitals.

The issues in reproductive care for Roma women are not unique to the Czech Republic and Slovakia. Ana Rozanova from the ERGO Network, a group of pro-Roma NGOs across Europe, told Index that women in these two countries have simply been more vocal.

This is just a snapshot into the wider discrimination faced by Roma women across Europe, based on both ethnicity and gender.

It is the women who have put an end to forced sterilisation in the Czech Republic and Slovakia by fighting for justice – but there is further to go. The rest must now come to light and be eradicated. ✖

Katie Dancey-Downs is assistant editor at Index on Censorship

ABOVE: Social media has become a megaphone for anti-vax conspiracies, making it harder for people with vaccine injuries to be heard

SPECIAL REPORT ◆ THE FORGOTTEN PATIENTS

An inconvenient truth

Stories of those who suffered injuries after receiving Covid vaccinations have been buried under a scourge of anti-vax misinformation, writes **ELLA PAWLIK**

VACCINES ARE ONE of humankind's greatest medical achievements. And, as with every drug that has ever been made, they can have side effects. It's not anti-science or anti-vaccine to say this. The co-existence of these facts means the mass Covid vaccination programme saved millions of lives and, inevitably, adversely affected a much smaller cohort of people.

Injuries vary from acute ones, such as vaccine-induced immune thrombocytopenia and thrombosis (VITT) – a dangerous condition involving clots in the blood vessels – to chronic ones such as vaccine-induced long Covid, which can cause a plethora of debilitating symptoms including extreme fatigue, pain and cognitive issues.

Overall, the benefits of vaccination far outweigh the risks. But what about the small minority who became ill or died after receiving the Covid vaccine – who listens to their stories?

Personal and clinical experience

Harriet Carroll was a Covid-19 clinical researcher in the UK's National Health Service. She was a member of the Sars-CoV-2 immunity and reinfection evaluation (Siren) study, a large NHS research project into the immune response to Covid-19 and vaccine effectiveness. She contributed to several papers exploring the benefits of vaccination and was one of the first in line in the UK to have hers.

But things took an unexpected turn

afterwards. "I had symptoms within a matter of hours," she told Index. These included numbness in her hands, dizziness, nausea, slowness, weakness and flu-like symptoms. Her tests, which formed part of the Siren study, offered clear evidence that her sudden illness wasn't caused by Covid-19 infection.

She was diagnosed with a hyperimmune vaccine response and has had myriad health issues including multiple pulmonary emboli, where blood clots block arteries in the lungs. Four years later, she still experiences multiple debilitating symptoms including fatigue, post-exertional malaise, insomnia and nausea, and is largely confined to her home. But she has struggled to get the medical help she needs.

Carroll has also met resistance in a professional capacity. In 2022, she was invited to submit a pre-recorded talk about translating evidence into clinical practice for an NHS Scotland conference on long Covid. She included her own experience of having been diagnosed with vaccine-induced long Covid after following NHS clinical pathways. She says she submitted it to her regional health board, NHS Grampian, for screening but it was rejected as she believes it didn't "toe the party line".

While she says her talk included only one "benign line" referencing the vaccine trigger for her long Covid, she said: "I genuinely think that they were super-anxious that this was some kind of propaganda to try to discourage vaccination."

The health board told her over email: "NHS Grampian does not currently have a 'party line' on post-vaccine long Covid. This needs to be done first, prior to any communication on the subject if we are speaking as NHSG representatives. Suggestion is to remove reference in slide to post-vaccine as this does not impact the overall recommendations provided."

Academia ignored

In 2021, a renowned biochemist in New Zealand – which had introduced vaccine mandates – was experiencing similar frustrations. Warren Tate is an emeritus professor of biochemistry at the University of Otago and a researcher in myalgic encephalomyelitis (ME). "I've always been pro-vaccination," he told Index.

Having observed adverse Covid vaccine reactions for ME patients through his study group and self-reported online surveys, he stipulated that there were more than 20,000 people in New Zealand vulnerable to the effects of the vaccine, and wrote to the government requesting vaccine exemptions. He also submitted an evidence-based paper on vaccine injury risk. While he says he initially received a "very gracious reply", ultimately his concerns were not acted on.

In the USA, researchers have been unable to publish work on vaccine injury. Using data from the Yale Listen Study, they released two papers: one on long Covid and another on post-vaccine syndrome. The papers had comparable datasets, and identical methodology and data analysis. The long Covid paper was published without hesitation, but the vaccination paper never made it past the pre-print stage.

David Putrino, director of rehabilitation innovation at Mount Sinai Health System (the largest hospital network in New York City), was one of the researchers. He says that despite the post-vaccine syndrome paper clearly emphasising the net benefit of Covid vaccination, they could not get it peer reviewed "due to stigma and optics".

Silenced realities

Online censorship of people's vaccine reactions is commonplace. Charlet Crichton, who gave a witness statement at the UK Covid Inquiry, was in hospital with a severe Covid vaccine reaction. She says that her medical consultants submitted 12 reports through Yellow Card – the online UK government service where people can report issues with medicines or vaccines. She started posting about her experiences online. "I got my first account warning by Facebook and I was told that if I posted anything like that again then I would be banned," she said.

Crichton set up a charity, UKCVFamily, for the Covid vaccine-injured and bereaved, to provide a safe space for people to share their experiences and support each other. "We don't allow any posts that are deemed anti or pro-[vaccine]," she said. But despite the group's neutrality, it has still been censored online.

"We had an account warning because of a BMJ [British Medical Journal] article that was posted about vaccines," she said. A poll of UKCVFamily members found that 74% had been censored when talking or posting about their adverse reaction to vaccines online. Relegated to the communication style of a criminal operation, the members started speaking in code instead, using emojis and abbreviations to work around the algorithms.

Even official communications regarding vaccine injury, such as evidence to the UK Covid Inquiry, have not been spared from censorship. Anna Morris KC, who represented UKCVFamily and other vaccine-injured groups, noted that "censorship has continued years after the pandemic", adding that YouTube had removed a video featuring her legal →

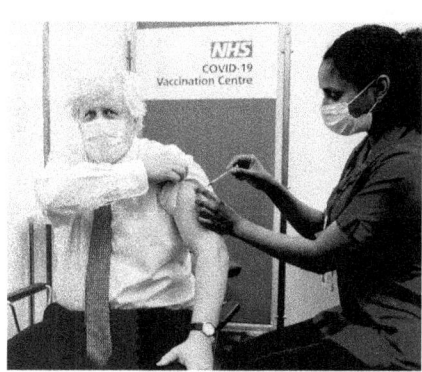

ABOVE: Former UK Prime Minister Boris Johnson receives his Covid booster jab at St Thomas's Hospital in London in December 2021

ABOVE: Former UK health secretary Sajid Javid arrives at Dorland House in November 2024 to give evidence to the Covid Inquiry

→ submissions to the inquiry in 2023. Despite requests for review, YouTube cited a violation of its "medical misinformation policy" as grounds for removal.

Another issue has been the government self-censoring in order to encourage vaccine uptake. In her closing speech at the inquiry, Morris highlighted that government messaging had favoured "speed and simplicity" over "transparency". She also pointed out that pathways to reporting vaccine injuries were inadequate: "The Yellow Card system was poorly known about, even amongst healthcare workers, and in 2021... not even the health secretary, Sajid Javid, knew about it."

Inconvenient truths

Being silenced can give those impacted the impression that they're victims of a big conspiracy – an understandable but inaccurate conclusion. The reasons are far more complex.

Much of the censorship is born of good intention to reduce vaccine hesitancy. Or, as Putrino said: "Folks often engage in cover-ups like this because they think that they're doing something for the greater good."

Valid questioning of Covid vaccines was discouraged to avoid it hampering what seemed like the only way out of endless lockdowns and restrictions.

Dr Asad Khan is a former NHS respiratory consultant who has had long Covid since contracting the virus in November 2020 while working. He then found himself bedbound after some of his symptoms got worse following the vaccine in February 2021. He has thoughts on the unquestioning religiosity surrounding vaccines. "They're the most effective group of drugs in history in terms of the amount of death and devastation that they have spared us... so I think that's where the worship comes from."

But there is a less benevolent reason for hushing up vaccine injury – no one wants to take responsibility for it. Morris's closing speech to the UK inquiry acknowledged that the government acted quickly to secure a "safety net" for pharmaceutical companies to protect them against the risk of litigation from adverse reactions, but did not provide a safety net for the people who suffered those reactions.

The rise in anti-vax misinformation online has also made it much more difficult for those with genuine injuries to tell their stories, as it has inhibited empathy and critical thinking.

"People worry that if they acknowledge there's a problem it will embolden and empower anti-vaxxers," said Putrino.

Social media has become a megaphone for those who "believe in conspiracies and who've done a lot of damage, [when] none of their arguments are based in science," added Khan.

Organised disinformation – the intentional spread of false information – was already happening before the pandemic, as one 2018 PubMed Central study on "weaponised health communication" indicated. It looked at how Russian trolls and Twitter bots were being mobilised to intentionally stoke division in the vaccine debate.

The side effects of silence

Ironically, attempts to censor the realities of vaccine outcomes to encourage uptake may have actually created more vaccine scepticism.

"The lack of support for genuine vaccine injury is massively feeding into vaccine hesitancy and anti-vaccine rhetoric," said Khan. However, he also acknowledges that it is difficult for governments to communicate that vaccines are safe and effective for most people, but that there can be adverse events for others.

For the injured and bereaved, it can feel as if nobody believes them. "We live our reality every day," said Crichton. "Yet society, public health [professionals], doctors, government, even friends and family say our reality is wrong."

And this can have tragic implications. Crichton says that since August 2022 more than one member of UKCVFamily has taken their own life, and 76% of members have contemplated it since their adverse reaction to the vaccine. She believes that "censorship has had a massive part to play in that" as "it has socially isolated and further stigmatised a marginalised and vulnerable group".

"If you can't talk to your peers, your friends, or talk freely in society about your real, lived experience then that has a really detrimental effect on not only your own personal health but also on the rest of society," she said. ✖

Ella Pawlik is a freelance journalist and copywriter

> **People worry that if they acknowledge there's a problem it will embolden and empower anti-vaxxers**

CREDIT: Wiktor Szymanowicz / Alamy

SPECIAL REPORT ◆ THE FORGOTTEN PATIENTS

Punished for raising standards

A lack of protection for healthcare workers in Nigeria who speak out against corruption is widening the country's inequality gap, reports **ESTHER ADEPETUN**

WITH A GROWING population that now exceeds 200 million, Nigeria's demand for effective healthcare is immense – but the sector is critically underfunded. Less than 4% of the country's GDP has been spent on health in recent years, resulting in operational inefficiencies, the deterioration of medical infrastructure, health professionals migrating to other countries, and medical tourism, where wealthier Nigerians pay for healthcare abroad instead of at home.

This year, the health sector was allocated only 5.18% of the total governmental budget, which will further impact the provision of quality services and deepen disparities in access.

Last September, the World Bank approved a $1.57 billion loan for Nigeria, including $570 million to strengthen primary healthcare provision. This is one of many international funds provided to help improve the country's healthcare infrastructure. However, systemic failures including corruption divert essential resources away from those who need them most.

A recent report from Transparency International – a global coalition against corruption – highlights corruption as a barrier to effective healthcare delivery globally and indicates that $500 billion is lost to the problem annually. Nigeria ranks 140 out of 180 in its Corruption Perception Index, reflecting its pervasive nature within the country's institutions. In healthcare, corruption manifests in many ways, including organ trafficking and unethical transplants, counterfeit drugs and the diversion of humanitarian aid.

In north-east Nigeria, the illegal trade of Ready-to-Use Therapeutic Food,

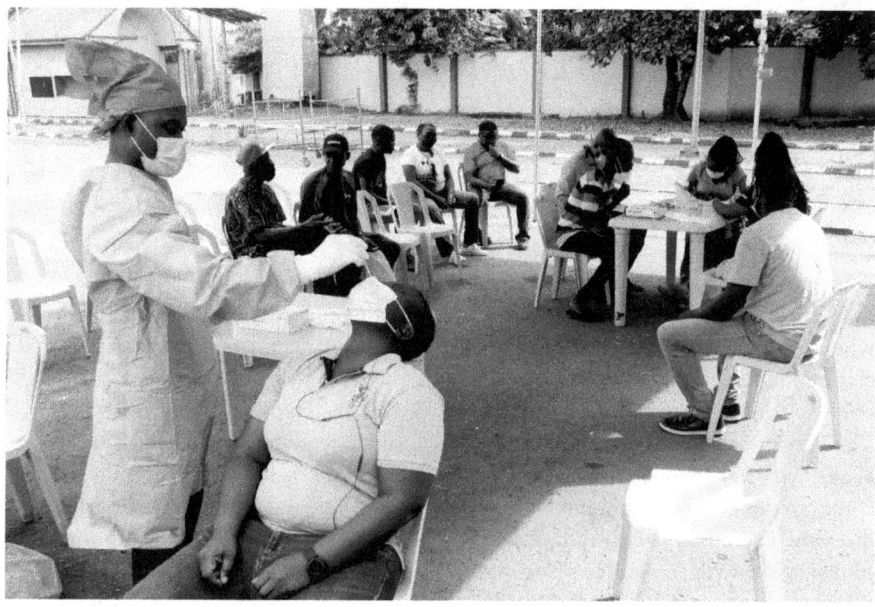

ABOVE: A healthcare worker collects swab samples from athletes for Covid-19 tests in Lagos, Nigeria in 2021

which is intended for malnourished children, highlights the severe misuse of humanitarian aid, with healthcare workers implicated in diverting supplies for sale in local markets.

Systematic financial abuse has also been documented by organisations set up to help Nigerians access affordable, quality healthcare. The National Health Insurance Scheme (NHIS), for example, allegedly misappropriated more than 6.8 billion Nigerian Naira ($4.5 million) through illegal allowances between 2016 and 2017. Despite its mandate to reduce out-of-pocket healthcare spending, the NHIS has managed to cover only 5% of Nigerians since it began in 2005, with the majority of Nigerians still financing their own healthcare through out-of-pocket payments.

A report by the news agency Sahara Reporters revealed rampant corruption at the National Hospital Abuja in Nigeria's capital, where patient-staff bribery and payments to private accounts are common. In another concerning account at a community health centre in Lagos, one →

> The failure to adequately protect whistleblowers leads to a deteriorating healthcare system and a loss of public trust

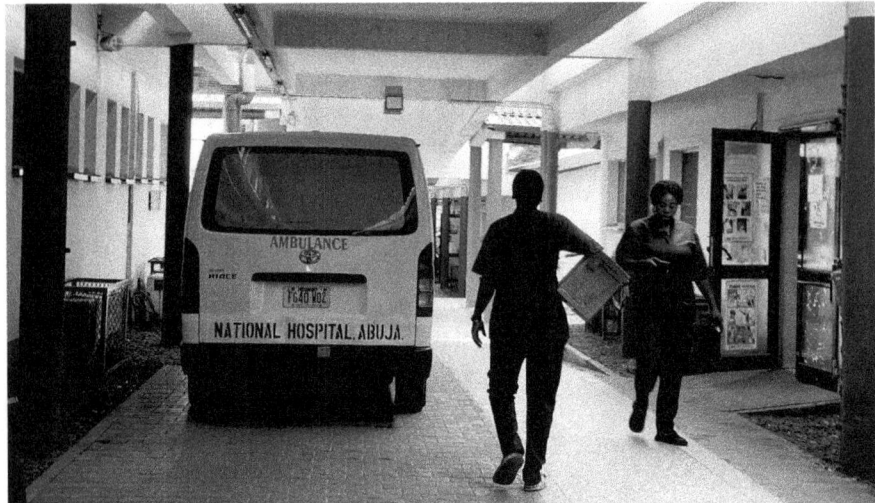

LEFT: An ambulance parked outside a ward of the National Hospital Abuja, Nigeria, where there have been allegations of corruption

→ anonymous healthcare worker told Index that contracted health workers who were paid to immunise young children had recorded discarded oral polio vaccinations as "administered". This distortion not only alters public health data but also places entire communities at risk of preventable diseases. There was also alleged misuse of resources, with the source reporting that solar-powered lights intended for use in healthcare centres were installed in the homes of local politicians instead.

Challenges faced by whistleblowers

Amid these challenges, whistleblowing has emerged as a critical strategy for combating corruption. Experts identify it as an accountability tool that can promote transparency and reduce corruption in healthcare service delivery. However, it is fraught with challenges, including intimidation, a lack of legal protection and a culture of silence. Whistleblowers endure significant personal risks, including emotional distress, underscoring the need for protective measures and a supportive environment.

A major shortcoming is the law. Onyinyechi Amy Onwumere, of the Civil Society Legislative Advocacy Centre (CISLAC), provides free, confidential and professional legal advice to victims and witnesses of corruption. She noted: "Nigeria does not have a comprehensive whistleblowing law. Existing protections are fragmented and insufficient, leaving whistleblowers vulnerable to retaliation.

"Whistleblowers in Nigeria's healthcare system often encounter retaliation, including threats, suspension or sacking, and even physical harm. These actions create a toxic atmosphere where human rights violations thrive, and potential whistleblowers are discouraged from coming forward.

"The failure to adequately protect whistleblowers leads to a deteriorating healthcare system and a loss of public trust."

There is also a lack of awareness among potential whistleblowers regarding their rights and the protections and reporting mechanisms that do exist, she added. According to the Centre for Fiscal Transparency and Public Integrity, a Transparency and Integrity Index the organisation compiled found that only 10 ministries, departments and agencies out of 512 in Nigeria have a whistleblower policy. "This is far from best practice," said Onwumere.

Cultural and systemic barriers

Cultural and societal norms create a challenging environment for whistleblowers. Informal corruption networks thrive where they are tolerated, particularly when they benefit the community. Tosin Osasona, a programme manager at the NISER/MacArthur Foundation Research Grant Project on Corruption Control in Nigeria, explained: "In a society where loyalty is highly valued, speaking out against one's institution can be perceived as a betrayal."

This attitude discourages people from stepping forward.

Osasona highlighted the professional risks that whistleblowers face. "They often encounter blacklisting by seniors, reduced future job prospects and ostracisation. The reality is that potential whistleblowers are intimidated, isolated and discouraged."

He stressed the need for a dedicated whistleblower reporting system tailored to the healthcare sector. "A reporting mechanism that guarantees confidentiality, independence, and impartiality is essential to breaking the cycle of corruption," he said.

One community health officer told Index that patients who were already burdened by the cost of treatment could find themselves extorted for basic medical services. They explained how a patient recently reported a staff member for selling injections that were meant to be free and for inflating the cost of other items. "Instead of facing disciplinary action, the individual was merely transferred to another clinic in the subdivision."

 Whistleblowers often encounter blacklisting by seniors, reduced future job prospects and ostracisation

And when staff members are the whistleblowers, they ultimately get transferred, "perpetuating a cycle of corruption and silence with no real change", the source added.

This climate of suppression extends to the media, where censorship continues to stifle investigative journalism – particularly on financial embezzlement. Despite amendments, authorities continue to misuse the broad powers of the 2015 Cybercrimes Act to detain and prosecute journalists uncovering corruption.

The path forward

There are severe consequences of widespread corruption in healthcare, including loss of life, increased healthcare costs and a deterioration of the health sector, disproportionately affecting vulnerable people.

Yusuff Adebayo Adebisi, a pharmacist and director of research and thought leadership at the international organisation Global Health Focus, said: "Corruption in healthcare resource allocation damages patient care. It deprives people who need treatment of crucial supplies and funding. This problem leads to drug shortages, outdated equipment and neglected facilities – all of which put patients at risk. Some people turn to expensive private clinics or skip treatment entirely because vital resources have been syphoned away."

A recent review from five English-speaking West African countries, including Nigeria, suggests that poor working conditions and low wages push some healthcare workers to engage in unethical behaviour. Adebisi emphasised that "a real solution calls for a detailed understanding of how corruption operates in each place so that decision-makers can craft effective strategies that address these problems at their core".

Empowering healthcare professionals to safely report corruption and mismanagement requires a combination of legal protection, secure reporting channels and a supportive workplace culture. Adebisi said that whistleblower protection laws are "essential" and should be communicated clearly to staff "so they know they will be shielded from retaliation". Secure, anonymous platforms – such as confidential hotlines or encrypted digital tools – can also help professionals speak up without fear of losing their jobs or facing harassment.

Training and awareness programmes on ethics and accountability can boost staff confidence. Adebisi suggested that "working with professional associations, non-governmental organisations and community groups adds an extra layer of support and helps create a culture where reporting is seen as a collective responsibility rather than an individual risk".

International models provide useful insights into how Nigeria can strengthen its whistleblowing framework. For instance, in the UK, National Health Service organisations rely on "Freedom to Speak Up guardians" who serve as neutral, trusted people who staff can approach with sensitive concerns. In some Latin American countries, partnerships between government agencies and civil society groups have led to digital whistleblowing platforms that maintain user anonymity. These ideas could be tailored to Nigeria, said Adebisi, taking into account the "unique challenges" of different regions.

Artificial intelligence can also enhance these efforts. He explained that "tools powered by machine-learning can track procurement data, pinpoint suspicious patterns in drug prescriptions and flag irregularities that might indicate theft or bribery". While technology alone won't solve the issue, he believes that integrating AI with "robust legal frameworks" and education programmes could help to "significantly strengthen oversight".

"There's no single solution that works for every institution, so it's important to combine strategies that promote accountability, protect staff and foster a culture of transparency."

A lack of accountability can have real-world consequences. One nurse in a teaching hospital told Index how corruption in resource management exacerbated existing disparities.

"Some wards are fully equipped with state-of-the-art machines, have a constant power supply and are staffed with highly efficient medical personnel," she explained. "Meanwhile, other units struggle with outdated equipment, erratic electricity and severe staff shortages."

When whistleblowers have the support of the media and the public, their reports can lead to meaningful reform. Onwumere highlighted the Ministry of Niger Delta Affairs scandal, where a whistleblower's revelations of looting at the ministry prompted policy changes. Similar pressure in the healthcare sector could drive accountability and bring change.

Ensuring that those who expose wrongdoing in healthcare can speak out freely is not merely a matter of individual rights – it is a critical step towards a functional and equitable healthcare system for the tens of millions of Nigerians who depend on it. ✖

Esther Adepetun is a journalist based in Nigeria

54(01):81/83|DOI:10.1177/03064220251332636

ABOVE: A pharmacy in Lagos, Nigeria. Crucial medicine is often misallocated in Nigeria through corruption and bribery, leaving many without necessary treatment

SPECIAL REPORT • THE FORGOTTEN PATIENTS

Nowhere to turn

ZAHRA JOYA reports on the dire state of women's healthcare and maternity services in Afghanistan under Taliban rule

OVER THE PAST 15 years, Bibi Jan has already endured the unimaginable pain of losing four of her children due to malnutrition and inadequate medical facilities. She is now deeply anxious about the health of two of her three surviving children.

I met the 30-year-old in December 2024 at the Zabul Provincial Hospital. I found her sitting beside her two sick children, aged six and three, her face etched with worry. She spoke in a trembling voice.

"Each of [my children] passed away after reaching six months or one year of age," she told me. "Now, my two other children are also sick. I brought them to this hospital for treatment. The doctors have admitted them. I am staying here while my husband visits us during the day and returns home at night."

Bibi got married when she was only 15 to a man who was 15 years her senior. "My father gave me away in marriage when I did not consent," she said. Since then, she has given birth nine times, but only one daughter and two sons have survived.

The women and children's ward of the hospital was so overcrowded that it was nearly impossible to find any space. Every bed was occupied, and some patients were sharing a single cot or lying on the floor, waiting desperately for medical attention.

Sitting next to Bibi was another woman, 37-year-old Fatima, who had brought her two-and-a-half-year-old child in for treatment. "Due to a lack of sufficient food, my children suffer from malnutrition and one of them is severely ill," she said. "We barely have anything to eat at home, let alone access to proper medical care."

The tragic accounts of Bibi and Fatima are just two of countless stories that reflect the dire humanitarian crisis in the southern province of Zabul. Women and children in this province face life-threatening health risks daily. The Zabul Provincial Hospital, which is the only major healthcare centre in the region, is grappling with critical shortages of medicine and medical equipment.

One of the doctors at the hospital, who preferred to remain anonymous, described the grim reality of their struggle: "We are trying to save patients' lives with the minimal resources available, but we lack adequate medicine and equipment. Foreign aid is not distributed properly, and most of it goes to specific Taliban-affiliated groups. Ordinary people, especially women and children, are deprived of this aid."

The drastic reduction in international aid following recent political changes has plunged Afghanistan's healthcare system into an unprecedented crisis. This includes both the reduction of government healthcare assistance within the country since the Taliban's takeover and recent reductions in foreign aid, particularly from Donald Trump's administration in the USA and his cuts to United States Agency for International Development (USAID) funding.

Organisations that once provided crucial support to medical centres in Zabul have either suspended their assistance or significantly reduced the resources they provide. Meanwhile, the Taliban lacks the capabilities and infrastructure to manage this growing catastrophe, and has actively enforced policies that make healthcare access harder.

A worsening nationwide problem

According to the United Nations Office for the Co-ordination of Humanitarian Affairs (OCHA), Afghanistan has a maternal mortality rate that is nearly three times the global average – for every 100,000 births, 600 women die.

In a recent report, the OCHA warned that this year nearly half of Afghanistan's

 We barely have anything to eat at home, let alone access to proper medical care

ABOVE: Mothers and babies who suffer from malnutrition wait to receive help and check-ups at a clinic run by the UN World Food Programme in Kabul in 2023. Malnutrition rates in Afghanistan are at record highs

population – or 22.9 million people – will require humanitarian assistance just to survive. The report also stated that 14.8 million people, more than a third of the country's population, will face acute food insecurity by early 2025.

This crisis extends far beyond Zabul. The Abu Ali Sina Balkhi Provincial Hospital in Balkh is also overwhelmed by the growing number of patients and the worsening economic situation.

At about 4pm one afternoon, a sudden commotion erupted in the overcrowded hallways of the hospital. A 42-year-old man, visibly pale and weak, was lying on a stretcher. He was a roadside vendor who had earned no income that day. His blood sugar levels had spiked dangerously high, leaving him unable to move.

His 12-year-old son and a coworker, both visibly distraught, had rushed him to the hospital. Despite the doctors' immediate attention, his condition was too severe for him to be saved. About 20 minutes later, a doctor's voice emerged from his office: "The patient has passed away."

Hospital officials then turned to his young son and requested that he contacted a family elder to collect the body.

Many of the patients seeking treatment in hospitals across the country have lost their jobs, struggle with chronic illnesses exacerbated by economic hardship, or suffer from the psychological toll of Taliban rule. Additionally, cases of suicide among women, driven by social issues such as domestic violence and forced marriages, have been steadily increasing.

Taliban restrictions further endanger healthcare access

The OCHA has expressed serious concerns over the increasing restrictions imposed by the Taliban on women's employment and education in the healthcare sector. These policies have drastically limited access to essential medical services for mothers and children across Afghanistan.

According to the OCHA, the country's economy has shrunk by nearly a third since August 2021. The ongoing political crisis, an inefficient financial system, severe cuts in development budgets and Taliban-imposed →

→ restrictions have seriously damaged the country's ability to deliver basic services.

The organisation highlighted the alarming maternal mortality rate during childbirth in particular, emphasising that the Taliban's restrictions on women working in healthcare have made access to medical care increasingly difficult.

In addition to these policies, last year the Taliban also banned women from studying in medical institutes, further depleting the already inadequate number of female healthcare workers and stopping them from being able to train in professions such as nursing, midwifery and dentistry. These were some of the only educational avenues left for women.

The desperate need for female doctors

In Badakhshan province, women are particularly affected by the shortage of female doctors. Fatima, a 24-year-old woman, expressed her deep concerns: "I always accompany my relatives who come from remote areas to the central hospital in Badakhshan because they don't know the way. The situation is truly worrying. There are so many patients but not enough female doctors. We must wait for hours just to get seen by one."

She recounted the harrowing experience of one of her neighbours who suffered severe complications due to a lack of doctors.

"Several specialised doctors we had have all left the country," she said. "My neighbour had to undergo surgery in the absence of specialists, but due to severe bleeding she had to go through another surgery within a week. She nearly died."

Dr Noshin Gohar Karimi, who works at Faizabad Provincial Hospital, voiced similar concerns on his Facebook page: "The workload in Faizabad Provincial Hospital has exceeded the capacity of

ABOVE: Taken more than 20 years ago, this photo shows women and girls attending a former maternal and newborn health station in Rawasha

the staff. Unfortunately, due to a lack of budget, increasing bed capacity and staff recruitment are not possible. The hospital was originally designed for 128 beds, but today more than 310 patients are admitted. In the paediatric ward, which has only 30 beds, 120 sick children and their mothers are currently being treated."

The healthcare workforce crisis

The shortage of medicines and lack of funding remain among the most pressing challenges in Afghanistan's healthcare system. A nurse at a government-run, public hospital in Kabul highlighted the ongoing crisis: "We used to have more staff, but over the past two years the workforce has decreased significantly. Now, one person has to do the work of several people and, as a result, patients do not receive adequate care. In addition to that, doctors and nurses face persistent delays in their salaries."

She added: "Before the Taliban took over, medical equipment was already scarce but, after that, even that small supply stopped. Many machines have become old and worn out, and hospital officials say they have no budget to replace them."

A nurse at a private hospital in Kabul also reported severe staff shortages in various departments. "There is a lack of personnel in all sections. In the nursing department, especially, we do not have enough staff and are forced to do the work of several people alone, while our salaries have also been reduced."

With a collapsing healthcare system, increasing restrictions on women and dwindling international aid, Afghanistan faces a healthcare catastrophe that threatens the lives of millions. ✖

Zahra Joya is an Afghan journalist living in London and editor-in-chief and founder of Rukhshana Media, a news agency reporting on life for women and girls in Afghanistan

Additional reporting by Rukhshana Media reporters

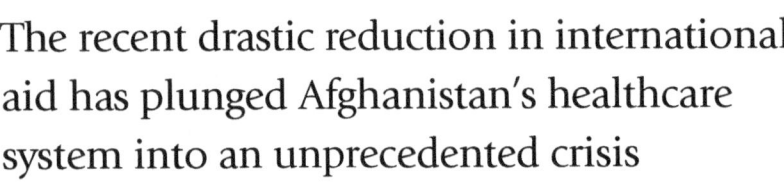

The recent drastic reduction in international aid has plunged Afghanistan's healthcare system into an unprecedented crisis

SPECIAL REPORT

SPECIAL REPORT ◆ THE FORGOTTEN PATIENTS

Emergency in the children's ward

Venezuela's healthcare system is failing young people and those who speak up are punished, writes **SHAYLIM CASTRO VALDERRAMA**

ABOVE: Venezuelans protest the lack of supplies, medicine and water outside the José Manuel de los Ríos children's hospital in Caracas, Venezuela, in 2020

IN VENEZUELA'S PRECARIOUS public health system, most patients must pay for everything: medicines, tests, gloves, syringes… the list goes on.

This is in spite of the constitution proclaiming a guaranteed right to health, for which the state is responsible. However, people struggle daily and speaking up has consequences.

Children and their mothers are among the most vulnerable, and Huníades Urbina-Medina, a paediatrician and president of Venezuela's National Academy of Medicine, has witnessed this firsthand.

With 35 years of experience in the health system, including at José Manuel de los Ríos Hospital (known as JM), the country's leading children's hospital in Caracas, he recalls a chilling incident from 2013.

That year, he took the mother of a young patient with kidney disease to a radio interview to discuss the lack of medical supplies. Although she spoke anonymously, she feared retaliation, and when Urbina-Medina tried to drop her off at the hospital afterwards she asked to get out several streets away.

"She confessed to me that she had been threatened. She said that if [hospital staff] saw her getting out of my car, they would remove her child from the hospital," he told Index, adding that this order would likely have come from the hospital management with the agreement of the government.

He said those making the threats were an armed militia group who watched the hospital. This group and *colectivos* – paramilitary groups which support the government – at one time did this to prevent protests and stop the press getting inside. Although they are no →

CREDIT: Associated Press / Alamy

When you complain, you expose the inefficiency of Venezuela's healthcare system

longer common, anonymous sources told Index there were still "spies" inside.

In that same year, Urbina-Medina says he received a "retirement letter".

"I talked a lot [with the media] and bothered the regime," he said. As he was a professor at the hospital and managed the postgraduate programme, he was able to continue. Despite this and other attempts to silence him, he is not afraid to speak out.

One particular area of healthcare has steadily fallen further into crisis in recent years. In 2017, the government-run Venezuelan Foundation for Organ, Tissues and Cell Donations and Transplant suspended its organ procurement system. Officials cited a shortage of immunosuppressants – drugs needed to prevent transplant rejection – and claimed the suspension would last three months. Eight years later, the system remains paralysed.

The body of one donor could save up to six people, and in 2021, a group of 12 teenagers awaiting transplants spoke before the Inter-American Commission on Human Rights about the crisis affecting children's and adolescents' health.

During the online hearing, the group – wearing face masks – demanded better nutrition, denounced the lack of health workers and called for the reactivation of the organ procurement system.

Two months later, one of the speakers, 15-year-old Niurka Camacho, died while waiting for a transplant. She is one of the 89 children and teenagers who have died since the system was stopped, Prepara Familia – an NGO that supports mothers and their children needing transplants – told Index.

Meanwhile, the Ministry of Health has not published any epidemiological data or health-related reports since 2016.

"When you face uncertainty, when you don't have medicines, people turn to foundations, organise raffles… they do a lot of things because these are high-cost medicines," said Evelyn Alonzo, general manager of the National Transplant Organisation of Venezuela (ONTV), an NGO that helps families obtain medical supplies and tests.

On average, a family waiting for a transplant can spend up to $250 a month on medicines, treatment and medical exams, according to Lucila Cárdenas de Velutini, the director of ONTV. This is in an oil-rich country where there is rocketing inflation and the official minimum wage is less than $4 per month.

After years with a chronic shortage of food, medicine and hygiene products, Venezuela – which ranks 19th out of 21 countries in the Americas for freedom of expression, according to Article 19's Global Expression Report 2024 – is also facing a humanitarian crisis, which is forcing more than 7.7 million people to flee the country.

"When you protest, [security forces in hospitals] intimidate you and you have to be quiet. That's why you don't see many protests anymore – they can [say to patients], 'We can kick you out'," Urbina-Medina said.

Despite these threats, at least 408 protests demanding the right to healthcare took place across the country in 2024, according to the Venezuelan Observatory of Social Conflict, an NGO focused on defending the right to peaceful protest. In the same year, police repression increased, especially after people took to the streets demanding transparency following a contested presidential election in July – the results of which remain disputed.

"When you complain, you expose the inefficiency of Venezuela's healthcare system," Urbina-Medina said.

According to two doctors who requested anonymity for fear of reprisals, there is another way that the authorities silence protest in the short term. State-controlled institutions such as the Ministry of Health and the Venezuelan Institute of Social Security will give patients medicine for just a few days. This is medicine that should be provided by the state, in an ongoing capacity.

"They only give you enough to keep you quiet for a little while," one of the doctors said. After this, patients need to find the money to use private institutions or get help from NGOs.

More than half the patients at JM de los Ríos Hospital come from outside Caracas. In 99% of cases, paediatric patients are accompanied by their mothers, who often must leave their jobs to care for their children, according to a 2023 Prepara Familia report.

"When a child is sick, a parent, an aunt, a grandmother, a nephew, a sibling quits their job to take care of the child during their dialysis or hospitalisation. That means a child is out of school and a parent or any other family member is out of the workforce," explained Cárdenas.

Although several organisations were willing to help children and their families with their medical needs, doctors said that some public hospital directors rejected outside help because accepting it would be "recognising that the state is not covering its responsibility". In general, directors of state-controlled institutions must be loyal to the ruling party. Those who are not risk being removed from their positions.

The ideal health system would be efficient, reducing the need for patients to fight, complain or protest in the first place. Until that time, Cárdenas says protests are vital for keeping the issue in the spotlight and ensuring that the call for equal and accessible healthcare does not go unanswered. ✖

Shaylim Castro Valderrama is a journalist based in Venezuela

COMMENT

"No one wants trial by the media, but it is vital that in the age of the internet, the courts strike the right balance between ensuring a fair trial and freedom of expression"

FREE SPEECH V THE RIGHT TO A FAIR TRIAL | GILL PHILLIPS | P.96

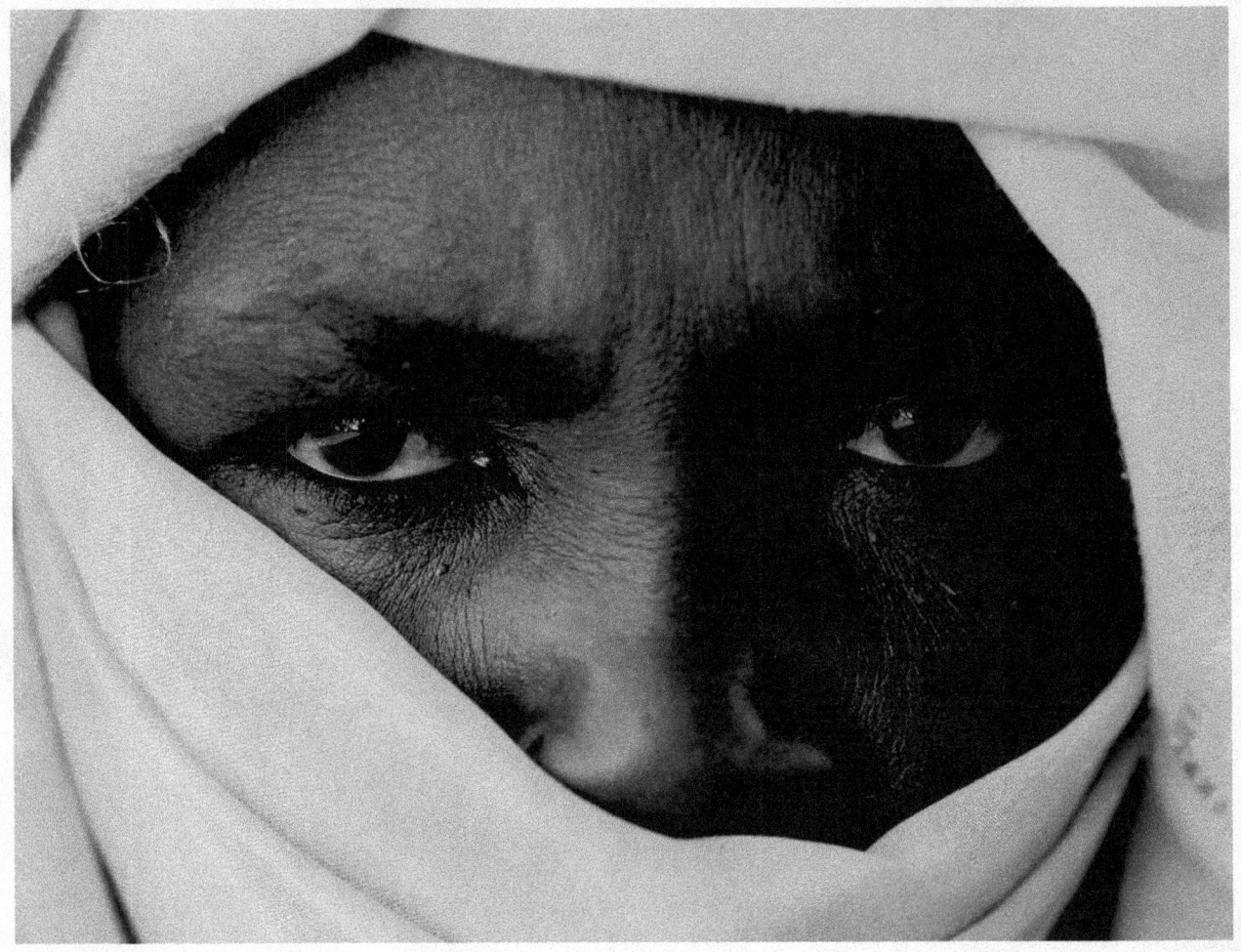

We need to talk about Sudan

The lack of debate surrounding the war in Sudan suggests that there is little global interest in the atrocities being committed, writes **YASSMIN ABDEL-MAGIED**

I RECENTLY ATTENDED AN interview with the Egyptian-Canadian writer and journalist Omar El Akkad ahead of the publication of his book, One Day Everyone Will Have Always Been Against This.

The book was born from a viral tweet sent shortly after bombardment began in Gaza in October 2023. El Akkad wrote: "One day, when it's safe, when there's no personal downside to calling a thing what it is, when it's too late to hold anyone accountable, everyone will have always been against this." The post was viewed more than 10 million times.

More than 150 people warmed the room on a cold London night to hear him speak. By the time I reached the front of the signing line, all copies of his book had sold out. *Alhamdulillah* (praise be to God), I thought, agreeing with his publisher's comments that this was a vital message, a critical meditation, the needed challenge for Western

ABOVE: A close-up of a Sudanese rebel in Darfur, Sudan. Despite decades of violence and atrocities in the region, many outside of Sudan remain unaware of the conflict

readers to grapple with their nations' complicity in what has been termed the "first live-streamed genocide".

Yet, despite the sharp clarity of El Akkad's words, the truth of his analysis and the profound power of his critique, I was unable to remain entirely present during the discourse.

Alongside my complete and lifelong solidarity with the Palestinian people, the feeling that kept interrupting was one I did not want to engage with, one I had no sense of how to acknowledge.

Would people ever one day "always have been against" the war in Sudan?

What does the answer to that question tell us? About Sudan, about the value we place on human life, about ourselves?

El Akkad's writing, and the writing of many Palestinians and their allies, points to a truth about the war in Palestine that is distinct from the war in Sudan: the battle of narrative.

Part of the red hot anger, the betrayal that many in the West feel, arises from the "derangement" of politicians, leaders and news organisations, who continue to disseminate lies, mistruths and propaganda about the war, despite positioning themselves as paragons of moral virtue and truth.

Sudan's challenge is different. There is no battle of narrative. There is an utter lack of narrative. People are "already against this", but it doesn't seem to matter enough. There is an utter dearth of interest in the deaths of hundreds of thousands of us, the genocide being committed as I type these words, the millions facing acute hunger, and the many millions more displaced.

I am reminded of the death of a marriage. When there is an argument there is the hope for progress, because at least the parties are engaged with each other. When there is silence, when all sides have left the table, then you know the battle is lost.

Sometimes, a dark, shameful part of me wishes there was a battle of narrative I could engage in. Maybe it would mean Sudanese lives mattered enough to fight about.

At this point, I feel I must issue a disclaimer. Our causes are not in competition with each other, and freedom is not a zero-sum game. Talking about Sudan does not – must not – come at the expense of talking about Palestine, and we must also be wary of those using the Sudanese cause to diminish the activism and agitation of Palestinians and their allies.

Perhaps this is one battle of narrative Sudan has unwittingly found itself in, used as a pejorative talking point in the same way those defending Muslim women's right to wear the hijab are faced with accusations that they "don't care about the women in Iran". These are bad faith arguments that are unconcerned with the actual people in question.

So why begin a piece about Sudan by talking about Palestine at all? Partly, I suppose, to start to try to make sense of a phenomenon I struggle with daily. To give those around me the benefit of the doubt; to resist the urge to point the finger and issue simplistic accusations forged in the blaze of desperation after years of being made invisible; to connect our struggles.

After all, there are no two flags as similar and as easily confused as Sudan's and Palestine's. We are distorted mirror images of one another, peoples so often frozen by the imaginations – or lack of imaginations – of others, refused the dignity of life as full, human beings who desire little more than peace and our freedom.

I had planned to feature more voices on the ground in this piece, yet the reality of the conflict once again interrupted any neat narrative I had hoped to write. My contacts in El-Fasher, the capital city of North Darfur, found themselves squeezed once again between heavy aerial bombardment by the Sudanese Armed Forces and shelling and drone attacks by the Rapid Support Forces, trapped between an exploding rock and a deadly hard place.

"I'm sorry for my late reply," came a recent message from one contact. "The local authority keeps shutting down the network." That was the last I heard from them, my questions languishing in the WhatsApp chat unread, "single ticked".

Another activist tells me she cannot bring herself to ask her contact to do an interview. She was panicking about feeding herself and not getting killed.

I feel ashamed, like a narrative vulture, picking at my people's bones.

In Khartoum, my aunt does not reply to questions about how she is doing. In the few moments of snatched connectivity, she forwards jokes and Arabic memes to the group chat. "I don't want to talk about this stinking war," she said. "Send photos of your cooking, of pretty hairstyles, of nice things." Joy, she said. That's what she wanted. Joy.

I am reminded of the bursts of joy I witnessed in the images of Palestinians returning to northern Gaza. Singing, laughter, jubilation… despite the dehumanising brutality, the Palestinians had what Omar El Akkad described as "the asymmetrical power of joy".

I think of this as another quality the Sudanese share with Palestinians – the asymmetrical power of joy. Unencumbered by our wrangling on moral positions, uninterested in the limitations of our imaginations. They continue to live. *Subhanallah*. Glory be to God. ✖

Yassmin Abdel-Magied is a Sudanese-Australian writer, journalist and broadcaster

There is an utter dearth of interest in the deaths of hundreds of thousands of us

RFK Jr could be a disaster for American healthcare

It is deeply troubling that the USA's new health secretary believes in conspiracy theories and is hostile towards modern medicine, writes **MARK HONIGSBAUM**

EVEN BEFORE THE Senate confirmed Robert F Kennedy Jr as US health secretary, the Trump administration was wreaking havoc with government agencies vital to medical research and equitable healthcare.

Ignoring Title IV of the 1964 Civil Rights Act, which prohibits discrimination based on race, colour or nationality, the White House removed swathes of data from the websites of the Centres for Disease Control and Prevention (CDC) and the Food and Drug Administration (FDA) overnight, in an effort to purge the agencies of what Elon Musk has dubbed "the woke mind virus".

Gone were vaccine guidelines for "pregnant people" and regulatory guidelines on increasing diversity in clinical trials. Even the Department of Veteran Affairs felt the impact of Musk and Donald Trump's anti-DEI (diversity, equity and inclusion) crusade, deleting advice on LGBTQ+ veteran care.

This was followed by a 90-day freeze and stop-work order on the United States Agency for International Development (USAID), jeopardising the lives of millions of people around the world who depend on its programmes for the prevention of diseases such as HIV, tuberculosis and malaria.

How precisely this will make America – or the world – "healthy again", to quote the slogan of Kennedy's MAHA (Make America Healthy Again) movement, is a question that he may now wish to ponder. In his new role as director of Health and Human Services – a $1.7 trillion agency with 80,000 employees – Kennedy will be responsible for everything from medical research and pandemic prevention to regulating the cost of medicine and health insurance for the poorest Americans.

On the campaign trail, Kennedy also promised to lift safety regulations on unpasteurised "raw" milk – a potential source of bird flu – and take a "break" from infectious disease research (including for Covid-19) by having the National Institutes of Health (NIH) pivot to chronic diseases such as diabetes.

But it is Kennedy's well-documented antipathy to vaccines that could have the most far-reaching impacts. Asked during the Senate Health Committee hearing whether he accepted studies debunking the theory that the measles, mumps and rubella (MMR) vaccine caused autism – a theory he has supported – Kennedy promised to be "an advocate for strong science", adding that "if the data is there, I will absolutely do that."

But for those who have followed the activities of Kennedy's Children's Health Defence non-profit closely, his efforts to roll back on previous anti-vax statements are not to be trusted. Indeed, even as Kennedy was testifying, a lawyer for Informed Consent Action Network – a non-profit whose founder is a close ally of Kennedy – was petitioning the FDA to revoke its approval of the polio vaccine. The vaccine is estimated to have prevented 20 million cases of paralysis globally and is widely regarded as one of the greatest achievements of US medicine.

Nor would Kennedy agree to sever his stake in ongoing litigation on behalf of people claiming to have been damaged by Gardasil, the Merck vaccine that protects against the human papillomavirus. According to financial disclosure documents filed ahead of his confirmation, Kennedy's arrangement with law firm Wisner Baum guarantees him 10% of payouts from successful Gardasil settlements – an arrangement from which he has earned more than $2.5 million in the past two years.

Ascertaining what Kennedy believes and understands by "science" is a fool's errand. As the editorial board of the New York Post concluded when it met him in May 2023, when it comes to medical issues his views are "a head-scratching spaghetti of what we can only call warped conspiracy theories".

> **It is Kennedy's well-documented antipathy to vaccines that could have the most far-reaching impacts**

The Committee to Protect Health Care, a pro-patients doctors' group, agrees. In a letter opposing Kennedy's nomination, it said that, as health secretary, his policies would hit vulnerable communities particularly hard, putting millions of lives at risk.

Kennedy is reportedly considering axing or changing a key vaccine advisory committee – a move that could prompt healthcare providers to offer fewer jabs to children and inspire states to repeal recommended vaccination schedules. According to the CDC, over the past 30 years childhood vaccines have prevented an estimated 1.1 million deaths and 32 million hospital admissions in the USA. The fear is that disruption to these schedules could harm community immunisation levels, which are already down on pre-pandemic numbers.

Just as worrying is Kennedy's record of aligning himself with propaganda films such as Medical Racism: The New Apartheid, which specifically targeted Black Americans to discourage them from getting vaccinations. In the past, Kennedy has suggested that Black people do not need to follow the same vaccine schedule as white people "because their immune system is better than ours" – a view that drew a stinging rebuke from Angela Alsobrooks, the Democrat senator from Maryland, during cross-examination.

Equally dangerous is Kennedy's record of intervening in public health crises. In 2018, he flew to Samoa to support a campaign that falsely suggested the MMR vaccine was unsafe. Several months later, a massive measles outbreak hit more than 5,700 people in Samoa and left 83 dead, most of them young children.

And during the Covid-19 pandemic he reportedly suggested that the coronavirus could have been "ethnically targeted" to spare Ashkenazi Jews and Chinese people

ABOVE: Robert F Kennedy Jr, the US Secretary of Health and Human Services, has expressed support many times for anti-vaccine views

– a claim that is both antisemitic and scientifically highly implausible.

During the hearings, Kennedy displayed a tenuous grasp of Medicaid and other US federal healthcare programmes he would oversee. In particular, he didn't seem to understand the role of community health centres, where many low-income Americans receive care, or that cuts to Medicaid would be particularly harmful to Black and Hispanic people, who are more likely than white people to be uninsured.

But perhaps the most revealing exchange came when Bernie Sanders, the independent senator for Vermont, asked Kennedy whether he agreed that healthcare was a fundamental human right. Kennedy's response that healthcare should not be treated the same way as free speech and that long-term cigarette smokers were "taking from the [insurance] pool" tells you everything about his eugenicist and libertarian mindset.

Listening to Kennedy's often-incoherent replies, it is hard not to conclude that he is someone who has studied a little medical history but has failed to absorb the lessons of germ theory or the role of social and economic conditions in determining health. Along with antibiotics, vaccines have saved more lives than any other technology in medical history. And while Kennedy's desire to wean Americans off processed foods would no doubt go some way to addressing chronic conditions such as obesity, his plan to remove fluoride from community water would not be helpful. On the contrary, his claims that fluoridation is connected to lower IQs is based on very flawed science.

Indeed, fluoridation is one of the most beneficial public health interventions in history. Prior to its introduction in the 1940s, Americans suffered from high levels of tooth decay. For those who cannot afford fluoride toothpaste or regular visits to the dentist, de-fluoridation would likely result in a surge in dental cavities. Not so much MAHA then as MATA – Make America Toothless Again. ✖

Mark Honigsbaum is a medical historian and journalist specialising in the history and science of infectious disease, and a senior lecturer in journalism at City St George's, University of London

The diamond age of death threats

In the relative anonymity of the online world, mudslinging has turned violent, writes **JEMIMAH STEINFELD**

OF ALL THE events that Index has run in my time at the organisation – from those on Tiananmen Square to others about cancel culture – it was not a talk on science that I expected to be the most controversial. How wrong I was.

Last October we launched our autumn magazine – which looked at the various ways scientists are censored – at the UK's Liverpool John Moores University. On the panel we had Paul Garner, professor emeritus in evidence-based public health in infectious diseases. In Garner's biography on the event flyer was this sentence: "Paul developed the post-Covid-19 condition and recovered using neuroplastic strategies."

We were unaware at the time that such a sentence was highly inflammatory. In the weeks leading up to the event we found ourselves in a storm.

For background, the post-Covid-19 condition is known colloquially as "long Covid". Garner suffered from it during the pandemic and wrote about his struggles. As part of this he said he'd developed empathy for those with myalgic encephalomyelitis (ME), a chronic illness that causes extreme fatigue and is little understood.

Those with ME are often frustrated by a medical establishment that they feel dismisses their symptoms. And Garner, too, felt he was being dismissed. Writing about this he became a hero within the ME community. The problem came when he underwent an intense programme – the "neuroplastic strategies" (such as mindfulness and meditation) referred to in his bio – which he believed lifted him out of his long Covid. When he discussed this publicly, he became persona non grata. He was not just shunned – he was subjected to death threats.

So when his name appeared as part of our event we were hounded and threatened, too, and had to get extra security.

No idea is sacred. All are up for debate, and we don't have to agree on everything. We also don't have to agree civilly. If someone wants to tell me that I'm an idiot for thinking Dirty Dancing is the best film of all time, so be it. People are entitled to their opinions and to their rage. But for free speech – the most sacred of rights – to work, there are lines… and sending death threats quite clearly crosses them.

Sadly, this isn't the first time recently I've come across topics that don't seem to be controversial (or at least that controversial) being met with extreme abuse.

Consider a few more: journalist Lewis Goodall was caught off-guard by a raging response when he announced his plans to travel to the Faroe Islands, whose reputation is chequered because of its whaling tradition. A researcher published a fact-based piece in The Lancet about the death toll in Gaza and got death threats – as did literature researcher Ally Louks after she shared a photo of her thesis title: "Olfactory Ethics: The politics of smell in modern and contemporary prose". US meteorologists feared for their lives simply for tracking the advance of hurricanes Milton and Helene.

But among the most surprising was the response to an article by Nadim Sadek in The Bookseller. Last October, Sadek argued that artificial intelligence could help the creatively challenged become better writers. He later told me that he'd have been "naïve to think that writing about AI at the moment, especially when there is an almost primal fear of it and its 'generative' capacity, would always be met with sanguine responses…" Still, he was shocked by the reaction.

"One said, 'Nadim Sadek should be held down by all the authors of the world and made to watch his family burn in his house'," he told me. "I mean, it's deeply unpleasant. These sorts of things can stir up a nasty momentum."

He was particularly upset by the way his children had to deal with it.

"They're powerless to protect me from this sort of thing and that impotence in the face of threatened death really made them unhappy."

Some of the above examples I've read online; others I've been told about casually in passing – over coffee, at dinner, in a children's play centre – as if they're totally normal. The fact that people don't seem particularly alarmed is understandable – for years politicians and public figures, especially female ones, have experienced insufferable violence online and it's been normalised.

 No idea is sacred. All are up for debate, and we don't have to agree on everything

ABOVE: We've reached a new era where vitriol appears to be rampant online, writes Jemimah Steinfeld

In 2014, for example, Reuters columnist Jack Shafer wrote an article crediting the internet with creating a "golden age of death threats". He gave examples of actresses, writers, tech executives, professional athletes and even video game designers who had received such threats, and wrote: "Advanced technology has removed most of the work and hazard from sending cowardly messages to people to frighten them."

Five years later, Vice published an article saying we had entered the "platinum" age:

"Some days in the Trump era, it can feel like death threats have become Americans' preferred way of communicating," it read. The list of victims was long and the article said "threats are so commonplace for members of Congress that news reports now describe them as a 'way of life'".

Today, with the net growing wider still, it's arguably time to coin it "the diamond age". Want further proof that this isn't just hyperbole? Google "Are death threats becoming more common online?" You'll be flooded with more recent examples.

From a cursory search, last year alone had German broadcaster Deutsche Welle running the headline "Digital death threats in sport: There's no space to run", coupled with the subhead "Cyberbullying has long been a problem for athletes on social media, but for many the issue is evolving into a more sinister reality".

US broadcaster NBC wrote: "Local officials increasingly targeted for threats and harassment, new data shows", and research reported on The Conversation said 74% of UK academics had received some form of extreme abuse online.

Who exactly is making all these threats? I'm almost too scared to ask. There's every chance, given we know so many people who receive them, that we might know people who make them.

That said, my curiosity gets the better of me and I go searching, only to find many articles on the victims and very little on the perpetrators, which feels like a problem in itself. It's important to understand the impact of the threats but it's also important to understand what impulses are driving those who are making them.

Let's stick with the impact, though. For the victims, the toll is unsurprisingly huge – both professionally and personally. At its most extreme, the stress for them has been reported to lead to hospital admissions and even suicide. For society, the impact is perhaps bigger still. People leave certain careers; others don't enter them at all. And all the while people are less vocal online, they self-censor, they don't engage in conversations, and our pool of those who are willing to speak becomes smaller and smaller.

While I'm unsure of what comes after diamond in the world of rankings, I can only imagine what it would look like online: a digital space where the only people left are those slinging threats at one another. An effective way to get them to taste their own medicine, perhaps, but not a race to the bottom that anyone should be part of. ✖

Jemimah Steinfeld is CEO at Index on Censorship

Free speech v the right to a fair trial

Legal consultant **GILL PHILLIPS** asks if the UK's contempt of court laws are fit for purpose in the digital age

LAST YEAR, UK readers found themselves unable to read an online article published by US magazine The New Yorker about the convicted murderer Lucy Letby. But this was not a straightforward case of online censorship – it was due to UK laws that prohibit or restrict the publication of potentially prejudicial material.

Contempt of court exists to protect all court and tribunal proceedings from interference, to safeguard the fairness and integrity of proceedings, and to ensure that orders of the court are obeyed. It comes in many forms, both statutory and under common law. Part of that law is based around "contempt by publication".

In the UK, for the purposes of reporting, a criminal case becomes "active" when someone is arrested, or a summons or warrant is issued. It remains this way until a defendant is sentenced or acquitted.

As journalism has increasingly moved online and become more international, it has become harder to strike the balance between freedom of expression (as established in Article 10 of the European Convention on Human Rights) and the right to a fair trial (Article 6).

Contempt laws cover a wide variety of conduct, including misbehaving in the courtroom ("scandalising the court"), refusing to answer a court's questions if called as a witness, and deliberately breaching a court order – but they also cover situations where journalists, bloggers or members of the public publish material that might risk prejudicing a trial. Some obvious examples would be publishing a defendant's previous convictions or implying that someone is guilty before they have been tried.

UK law on "contempt by publication" is primarily set out in the Contempt of Court Act 1981. This enacts what is known as the "strict liability" rule, which applies once criminal cases are active. At this point, any publication that creates "a substantial risk" that the course of justice will be "seriously prejudiced" will be in contempt. This "substantial risk" is assessed on a case-by-case basis.

In the Letby case, the New Yorker article was geo-blocked in the UK, although it could still be read in the print magazine.

Neonatal nurse Letby had been found guilty at a trial in 2023 of murdering seven babies and attempting to kill six others. She had been sentenced to a whole-life prison sentence.

At the time of the article's publication (May 2024), Letby was awaiting a retrial on one charge of attempted murder, scheduled for the following month. The judge put a series of reporting restrictions in place around what could be said about the original trial. There was concern that the New Yorker piece might breach those restrictions and prejudice the jury hearing the retrial.

Concerns about the impact of reporting on juries is a key part of contempt by publication. Judges are expected to be able to rise above what they read in the press – in 1960, a judge put it as such: "A judge is in a different position to a juryman. Though in no sense a superhuman, he has by his training no difficulty in putting out of his mind matters which are not evidence in the case. Jurors, on the other hand, are more likely to be influenced by what they read in the media and elsewhere."

When the 1981 act was passed, there was no 24-hour rolling global news, internet, social media or blogging. Publication was generally by printed articles in UK-based newspapers and news reports on television or radio.

In 2007, Richard Danbury, a former investigative journalist and now a senior journalism lecturer at City St George's, University of London, wrote a Reuters Institute report on this very topic, and described "the danger posed by the rise of the internet to the doctrine of contempt". "It risks becoming unenforceable," he wrote.

In 2011, in what was described as a landmark ruling for internet publishing, daily newspapers The Sun and the Daily Mail were found guilty of contempt over the online publication of a picture of the defendant in a murder trial posing with a gun.

Despite lawyers for both newspapers arguing that the risk of prejudice was "insubstantial" because

A legal framework that was intended to protect juries from prejudicial publication looks increasingly flimsy

ABOVE: Following the murder of three young girls in Southport in 2024, violent clashes broke out across the UK fuelled by the spread of racist misinformation online

the photo was quickly removed and jurors had been ordered not to conduct online research, the court concluded that the photograph created "a substantial risk of prejudicing any juror who saw [it]", adding: "Once information is published on the internet, it is difficult if not impossible completely to remove it."

Fast forward to 2025, and a legal framework that was intended to protect juries from prejudicial publication looks increasingly flimsy and ineffective when viewed against a backdrop of smartphones, echo chambers, citizen journalism and the dissemination of lies and disinformation by the rich and powerful on social media.

In recent years, in an attempt to manage the risk of contempt by publication, the UK attorney general's office has taken to issuing what it calls "media advisory notices" in high-profile cases, but these often just restate general principles and sometimes actually get the law wrong.

Unfortunately, we have ended →

up with a two-tier system in which the mainstream UK media (which are generally respectful of the law) is often seriously restricted in what it can publish while people on the fringes of the wild web are spreading the sort of (mis)information that the law is meant to be restricting. This is often published to a much wider – and more gullible – audience. As former attorney general Dominic Grieve commented in 2011, "the inhabitants of the internet often feel themselves to be unconstrained by the laws of the land".

Under the law, a publisher is liable for material legitimately posted online before legal proceedings become active, and which is then considered to be prejudicial once a case is active.

In practice, most UK publishers are careful not to link to old news reports within new reports of live cases about the same defendant, so the chances of a juror seeing possible prejudicial material are pretty slim. Jurors in the UK also now get very specific instructions from trial judges not to do their own online research, and in 2015 a criminal offence was introduced for jurors who do so.

However, this still effectively imposes an impossible burden on the media to monitor online archives to check whether they relate to newly-active legal proceedings. This task has become even harder since 2013, when the police decided to stop naming people who had been arrested, and instead name them only when they were charged.

A lot of these issues came to a head last summer after the Southport stabbings, in which three children were killed at a dance class in the north-west of England. Concerns were raised about the lack of official information available to counter misinformation spreading on social media about the attacks, and that misinformation was blamed for riots and violent protests across the country.

In the hours immediately after the stabbings, only a short statement was issued by police to say that "armed police have detained a male and seized a knife". This lack of public information appears to have been the result of a rather problematic combination of concern over contempt by publication rules, court-made privacy law around not naming suspects before charge, and statutory reporting restrictions around naming under-18s.

It is also hard to enforce contempt laws against articles that are uploaded outside England and Wales. As we know from the debate over online safety, domestic courts have struggled with extra-territorial jurisdiction when it comes to the internet.

So, what is to be done? In the digital arena, the protective approach towards court reporting in the UK seems to set too high a threshold, is imprecise and, operationally, ends up being over restrictive in some ways and ineffective in others. Our laws do not give sufficient credit to the robustness of the jury process. Juries must be trusted to reach verdicts on the evidence placed in front of them during the trial.

There is a need for a specific "public interest" defence where contempt by publication is alleged, which would allow for questions of proportionality and balance to be asked. There is also an argument to be made for moving the point at which criminal proceedings are considered "active" away from the moment of arrest and forward to the point of charge. This would be more consistent with the criminal justice process, as a charge is the moment when it is definite that there will be a trial.

This is not to say that the UK should move towards a US-style legal system, where freedom to publish can sometimes seem to take precedence over fair trial considerations.

In July 2024, the Law Commission – a UK statutory independent body – launched a wide-ranging consultation on contempt of court with a view to reform. The consultation initially closed in November, but last month a brief supplementary consultation paper was published (which closed on 31 March) as a result of issues arising out of the Southport attacks last year.

It warned of the growing conflict between contempt of court laws and public safety: "It has been suggested that the disorder was an indirect result of contempt of court laws: in constraining what information public authorities could disclose in relation to the defendant, contempt law helped to create an information vacuum in which misinformation, disinformation and counter-narratives could spread unchecked."

The Law Commission is expected to publish its initial report on liability for contempt (including contempt by publication, which will also address the issues raised in the Southport attacks) later this year.

No one wants trial by the media, but it is vital that in the age of the internet the courts strike the right balance between ensuring a fair trial and freedom of expression. ✖

Gill Phillips is a legal consultant and a former editorial legal director of The Guardian

The inhabitants of the internet often feel themselves to be unconstrained by the laws of the land

CULTURE

"People living in dangerous places – we still love to sing, to dance, and we do it with all these consequences and difficulties facing us. It becomes more beautiful"

WHERE IT'S MORE DANGEROUS TO CARRY A CAMERA THAN A GUN | ANTONIA LANGFORD | P.110

An unjust trial

Through powerful allegory, the human rights activist, playwright and novelist **ARIEL DORFMAN** reflects on the repercussions of denying the oppressed the space to tell their stories

UNSPOKEN

By Ariel Dorfman

"DON'T DO IT," her husband said. "I'm begging you not to go."

Annieke's only response was to tie her bonnet more firmly, making sure not a wisp of hair was visible.

Marius lowered his voice even more, so there would be no chance the man outside could hear them. People in the village were already suspicious of her comings and goings, her healings and visions. Gossip that she was a shrew, a disobedient, rebellious wife was what the family least needed right now.

"Think of the danger," he said. "Van der Pol hates you. He has been waiting for this chance. Think of that."

She turned to him, looked into his sad, alarmed, lovelorn eyes. "I am thinking of those creatures," she said. "They are the ones in danger, that cat and that dog, not me. They are the ones to be burnt alive if I do not go."

"The children, then," Marius said. "Think of our children."

"I think of them all the time. If they were old enough, they would understand."

"Promise me, Annieke," Marius said, "promise me that you will not do anything foolish, that you will hold your tongue."

For the first time since Meneer Gropius had come to ask for her services, she smiled. "It is not my tongue that matters here," she said. "But I promise. I will not do anything that you would regard as foolish. And now, I cannot keep tarrying. Justice does not wait for women like me."

"They will be benevolent," Marius said, "you will see."

She nodded, though it was unclear if it was because she agreed or disagreed with him or was simply saying good-bye.

Meneer Gropius was on the doorstep, examining his shoes, first one, then the other, as if he were concerned that there might be some dung clinging to them.

"Ah, Mevrouw Janssens," he said now. "Thank you for agreeing to expose yourself like this. My dear wife will be very appreciative, as will the kinderen."

"I am not doing it for her or for you or even for the young ones, bless their souls. I am doing it for God's creatures. They deserve the chance to be heard."

* * *

The hall where the court had convened was abuzz with murmur and chitchat but as soon as Annieke Janssens appeared, everyone fell silent. The three judges looked down on her from the podium.

"Ah," said the Hoofd Rechter. "About time. Now that Mevrouw Janssens has deigned to arrive, beautiful as ever, we can proceed. You may sit next to the culprits, woman. The closer you are to them, the easier it will be, I am sure, for you to translate how they intend to respond to the allegations brought against them. You are aware of what they have been accused?"

"Everybody in the village knows, sir," said Annieke, sitting down on a bench next to the two caged animals. "The dog has been charged with biting the ear of the eldest son and heir of the Van der Pol family in Church last Sunday. The cat, of showing glee at this action, meowing for joy as the lad was being attacked. And both of them are also imputed to have drunk from holy, consecrated water immediately afterwards."

"An impious, diabolical act," interjected Meneer Van der Pol, who was there both as aggrieved party and prosecutor. "And all of this has been established by many witnesses. Even you were there, Mevrouw Janssens or whatever your real name is, or will you deny what your own eyes saw when my boy was assailed; are you that brash and mendacious?"

Meneer Gropius raised his hand, humbly asked permission to speak. "Annieke Janssens is not here as a witness. My family is not contesting what happened on Sunday. I have asked her to come today so she may help my poor little →

animals explain why they acted in a fashion so unlike them, so the judges may have mercy on these creatures that my wife loves dearly, that have played with my daughters since they were born."

"Yes, yes, yes," said the Hoofd Rechter. "We have heard this already, we have heard testimony as to the good character of these animals. Let me be clear, however: you are not denying that the assault took place nor that they drank from holy water?"

"Who could deny what they did? It is only in the hope that we can understand the reasons that I have brought Mevrouw Janssens here; perhaps her intervention might mitigate their sentences."

"Annieke Janssens, you may speak."

Annieke stood up from the bench. "I am not the one who must speak. This dog, this cat, they are the ones who must speak. I cannot represent them until I have had a chance to listen to their story."

"And this is something that you know how to do, Mevrouw Janssens?"

"Your honour is aware of my modest talents. Did I not heal your horse last year?" She turned to the judge by his side. "And you, did I not help your sow to bear the piglets with little or no pain?"

"Not just animals," Meneer Gropius interposed. "Many of the most observant people of this village owe their health to Mevrouw Janssens: the herbs she gathers, her soothing words, the touch of her hands. The court cannot doubt her skills."

"The skills of a witch!" Van der Pol's voice was strident, his face red as he pointed a large finger at Annieke. "I have never used her services. She casts a spell and then receives a reward for lifting it. She is the one who should be on trial; she probably incited these animals to do their worst."

There were shouts from the public, some in favor of Annieke, others acclaiming her accuser.

"Silence, silence!" the Hoofd Rechter thundered. "As for you, Meneer Van der Pol, do you have proof to back up your claim?"

"I know what I know. Women like her, they hide their arts and wiles, they are careful to cover their tracks, they creep out at night to dance in the forest, naked and covetous. But here she is now, you will all be able to perceive in the light of day from where she derives her satanic power. She claims she can speak to the animals, though God in Heaven decreed they would be deprived of reason or a soul; they should occupy a lowly rung in the hierarchy of being. Alright, let her communicate, if she can, with this dog that bit my boy, tore off his ear, and with this cat; look at how it licks its paws as if mocking us, daring us to punish its transgressions. Let's see if it is in such cheerful spirits when the fire devours its limbs and the devils are forced to leave this mortal, foul body where they have lodged in order to do mischief."

Annieke sighed, made a gesture to the Hoofd Rechter with her hands, as if weary or dismissive or merely pleading, or perhaps all of these together. "Sir, how can these animals be expected to tell the truth if they are being threatened in this way? Could you ask Meneer Van der Pol to refrain from this sort of intimidation?"

"You think the dog and the cat know the content of Meneer Van der Pol's words?"

"They know everything we say. We are the ones who are unable to understand what they say. If I could be left to deal with them without interruptions, sir, I hope to have news from them soon."

"Go ahead," the Hoofd Rechter said. "And you are warned, Meneer Van der Pol. We understand that you are upset about the damage to your son and dismayed, as we all are, that the holy water in the fountain of our Church has been soiled by these beasts; but we must give the accused all the legal rights that they possess, as is customary according to our laws."

* * *

It took Annieke a while to calm the dog and the cat down. She hummed to one and purred to the other, she reached into their cages and caressed their heads, allowed them to lick her fingers, waited for their throats to trust her. A wave of

Women like her, they hide their arts and wiles, they are careful to cover their tracks

fear was what first slapped her like a blaze, fear of the bonfire that was looming with its hot, liquid flames, but also a deeper, more despairing fear that nobody would believe their version, attend to what they had to say. She had to convince them that it was worth the effort, that this was their one chance to speak out, that she would try to be as truthful in transmitting their story as any human could be, and to please forgive any mistranslation; something would inevitably be lost as she transferred into the limited human tongue the rich sensory experience of what it meant to be a dog, what it meant to be a cat. Gently, she coaxed from them what had happened, burrowed into their minds with all the intensity and kindness she could muster, saw the scene again, now from their perspective, let the mewls and woofs, the moans and whines, paint the picture, vividly enough so that she could represent them, no matter how inadequate her own articulations might be.

She quietly thanked the dog, thanked the cat, turned to the judges.

The lad, young Master Van der Pol, had been tormenting living creatures for many years now, ever since infancy. Stomping on anthills, cutting spiders to pieces, crushing the eggs of baby birds in their nests, felling trees that gave shade in the summer and fruit in the spring, pissing in the pools formed by the brook that ran behind the main road to the village; the boy was blind to the beauty and splendour of Nature. The dog and the cat had watched this patiently, waited for his father to teach the youngster that this was wrong. Instead, Meneer Van der Pol, perhaps because he was so rich and was himself abusive with the peasants who worked for him, had encouraged this behaviour, told his son that we have been given by God sovereignty over the realm of the plants and the kingdom of the animals to do with them what we will, if it gives us pleasure, if it serves our purpose.

At this point, Meneer Van der Pol interrupted with a protest.

"It is well known," he said, "that Annieke Janssens envies me my position as the most prosperous member of this community, is angry because I have refused to call her when one of my goats is sick or someone in the household is ailing. She reviles me for trusting in the Good Lord rather than in her devious magic and allures. And now here we have her, using this occasion to malign me, pretending that this is a message from these beasts when it comes from her own dark heart. Outrageous! She can no more understand what these dumb brutes are saying than I can. Unless what she hears derives from some demonic force. In any case, I demand that this mad woman desist from defamatory statements."

"Mevrouw Janssens, please confine yourself to the events of last Sunday."

"Last Sunday, agreed. The accused were outside the Church, happily awaiting the sounds of the mass, which they enjoy when they can, believing that our Lord Jesus Christ did not only resurrect to save mankind but also every creature on this earth of ours."

"Blasphemy," said Meneer Van der Pol, "to so denigrate our holy doctrine."

Annieke lifted her cross from her bosom, where it had been resting, bobbing up and down when she was agitated, reposing when she had been calming the animals down. She showed it now to the judges and then to the public and finally to Meneer Van der Pol.

"A century ago, in the year of our Lord 1226, there died in Assisi, far from our Low Countries, but close to our hearts, a saintly man named Francis. I say saintly, because he was canonised two years after his death by Pope Gregory. He spoke to the animals as if they were brothers and sisters, and preached to the birds. He listened to the grievances of a wolf that was attacking the people of Gubbio, convinced them to feed →

him and thus stopped the attacks, avoided bloodshed and sorrow. I am but an ignorant woman in a small village, married to a poor carpenter since the age of 13, unschooled except for what the flowers have taught me, but even I have heard of the acts of Saint Francis. And if he were here today," Annieke summed up her argument, returning the crucifix to her bosom, "it would not be necessary for someone like me to have responded to this summons."

"We are not here to discuss theology or Italian friars," said the Hoofd Rechter. "We are here to determine whether a crime has been committed and if so, what punishment should be meted out so that such conduct will not be repeated in the future. This court has found animals guilty when they have misbehaved, especially pigs; we have ordered pigs hanged in an exemplary way for assaulting our townsfolk and destroying crops, but we have also shown mercy when it has been proven that these creatures meant no malice or were justified in their actions. Let us proceed."

She explained that on Sunday the boy, young Master Van der Pol, had arrived at the Church earlier than most of the flock and had gone out of his way to kick the dog and spit at the cat, disturbing them as they rested in the sweet sun of that morning. The animals had done nothing to warrant such an incursion nor did they react to it, letting the lad disappear, unmolested, into the vestibule. They had then drawn near to the door, as they were wont to do on the Day of the Lord, to better absorb the sermon and the chants of the choir and the responses of the congregation, adding their own melodies and yowls and vibrations to the prayers of men, women and children. And in that providential activity they had been engaged when their tormentor crept out from the Church with a slingshot and, without rhyme or reason, had smacked them with several sharp stones, whereupon the affronted parties had been unable to contain their righteous anger and had taught him a lesson. The dog was acting more in indignation at the boy desecrating a holy space than out of a desire to redress any offence it may have suffered. The dog swears that it merely nibbled at the ear of the miscreant and is sorry

We are here to determine whether a crime has been committed

that the boy's stupid attempt to free himself from this just chastisement had led to blood being spilled. As for the cat's meows, they had not been of joy but rather of concern for the health of Master Van der Pol who, despite his cruelty towards them, was a fellow inhabitant of this fallen world and worthy, therefore, of care and attention. The cat freely admitted that it had been the one to suggest to its dog companion that they both lap up some water from the nearest source they could find and sprinkle the injured ear, only later learning that this came from a fountain that had been blessed by our Holy Mother the Church, an act for which they asked forgiveness, though they also were glad now that the water was hallowed, as that might help the boy's ear to heal all the sooner.

"And this convoluted tale," the Hoofd Rechter said, "you garnered from your exchanges with the defendants?"

"I translate what I hear, sir. They do not speak with words as humans do, but still they have much to say, a host of complex thoughts and feelings contained in gestures and eyes, infinite nuances in their growls and purrs. I have tried to convey what they lived through as well as I could, even if it is impossible for mortals to really step across the line that divides us from our friends in the animal kingdom."

"And what say you to this account, Meneer Van der Pol?"

"There is no corroboration for it, good sir, none at all. My boy has been known to misbehave, as boys do from time to time, but never in the ways that this sorceress has implied. And I can vouch that last Sunday he did none of the things she has imputed. He was with me and his mother when the events took place, from the moment the family arrived in Church until he was vilely attacked by this cur, urged on by that feline, which we all know is the preferred companion for witches and women of loose morals. Unless another witness were to come forward to attest to the absurd story she has concocted to get her partners in crime acquitted, I ask that the maximum penalty be applied and I receive compensation from the owners of these pets, so that the Gropius family keeps its animals under a tighter leash and most definitely keeps them away from Church on Sundays, if not all other days of the week."

"And you, Meneer Gropius, what is your response?"

"I am sorry for the damage done and willing, though we can ill afford it, to pay a fine, if the court will be so merciful as to spare these dear animals who, up till now, have never hurt anyone, and are the delight of my wife and kinderen."

"Very well. We will now confer."

Annieke stayed by the animals, murmuring to them as she watched the three judges whisper to each other, back and forth, her hand back and forth over the neck and back of the dog, of the cat, as the men who would decide their fate went back and forth, back and forth with their words that they thought only they could hear; that they did not know the animals could understand, so much so that both cat and dog were aware of the conclusions that had been reached before they were announced. She could tell this was so because something stiffened in the muscles of the dog, the throat of the cat clutched up, she was ready for what the Hoofd Rechter would declare before the words left his mouth.

"We have reached a verdict," the Hoofd Rechter said and the other two judges nodded.

* * *

Marius knew that something was wrong as soon as his wife entered the house, by the way she took off her shoes, placed them too deliberately in a corner by the front door, did not want to meet his gaze. He had learned that he must wait until she was ready to speak.

"The children?" she asked finally.

"Still with my mother."

"Good that I married a wise man," she said.

She went to the stove and smelled the vegetables cooking, the stew she had made early that morning when she expected that Meneer Gropius would come to ask for help that would stop her from that sort of chore the rest of the day. She shuddered at how much she enjoyed that succulent aroma, the steam rising and tickling her skin, the warmth of the logs, as if nothing had happened, as if everything could go on the same as before.

Without showing Marius her face yet, her back still to him, she said:

"They are dead. All that I managed was to spare them the fire, that pain, at least. And be by their side as they were tied and muzzled so they would not fight back and then hanged. I was allowed to stay by them as they died, one thing that proves the judges are not entirely heartless. Though I do not think they are partial to me, not at all."

"They...?"

"I was warned to be careful, that the judges and others had their eye on me, that they did not find my testimony valid and suspected that I had made up the account, that I should not expect them to be so lenient if I persisted in telling lies, claiming I could speak to animals, to be wary of appearing as if I were a saint, as the devil has many guises."

"And that is all?

"This is not enough?"

"Something else," he said, "there is something else."

"Nothing else," she said. "They are dead and I could not save them and I must be careful."

He knew that this was not all. He hoped she would be forthcoming later that evening, when the children were asleep and the bewilderment of her body was beneath or above his or afterwards; or maybe tonight there would be no celebration of their love, maybe it would be days before they were interfused in the enchantment of that embrace. Maybe they would have to wait until her eyes had lost their clouds and her skin →

its mist and the sorrows of today had been softened by time; then he hoped that she would tell him, confide in him as she always had.

This time, however, it would be different.

She could not tell him what the muffled howling of the animals portended as they were carried away to be hanged, forecast as the rope was tightened around their neck, what her hands felt and ears heard as they gasped their last.

She knew their prophecy would come true.

She knew that a day would come, many centuries hence, when what had been done that day would come back to haunt the descendants of the men who condemned this dog and this cat to death. She knew that this was just one profanation among many, that the animals were not the only ones to be murdered, that somehow – she did not understand how this could be so, but it could not be denied – the trees would be killed and the water poisoned and the very air every living creature breathes and the fish in the sea. Annieke's heart broke to think that if the verdict that afternoon had been of another kind, if those judges had been able to cross the frontier into the pulsating life of those being accused – she was filled with desolation when she thought that if they had only listened to the animals, then the apocalypse they had warned her of could have been avoided. But no. This was the vision she had inherited from the dead. The mistreatment suffered that day would be visited on many tomorrows. There would be all Hell to pay: fire and drought, famine and pestilence, ravaging waters and wind.

And none of this could she reveal to Marius or anyone else.

All she could do was to repeat the prayer she uttered while her friends were dying.

Marius listened as she got down on her knees by the bed where they conceived their children; he listened and tried to understand what revelation had come to her, he tried to understand and could not.

It was a psalm, that much he knew, the one that, according to what travelers and mendicants tell, St. Francis had asked to be read to him as he lay dying.

"I cried unto the Lord with my voice; with my voice unto the Lord did I make my supplication. I poured out my complaint to him; I showed before him my trouble. When my spirit was overwhelmed within me, then thou knewest my path. In the way wherein I walked have they laid a snare for me. I looked at my right hand, and beheld, but there was no man that would know me: refuge failed me; no man cared for my soul."

Marius wanted to tell her that she was not alone.

But maybe she was, maybe there was nothing that even he could do to relieve whatever ailed her.

"I cried unto thee, O Lord. I said, Thou art my refuge and my portion in the land of the living. Attend unto my cry, for I am brought very low. Deliver me from my persecutors, for they are stronger than I."

She stopped and then, gathering strength from who knows what dawn inside her long night of the soul, what birds high in the air above, she went on:

"Bring my soul out of prison, that I may praise thy name. The righteous…"

But she faltered, could not continue, could not end the psalm as she always had, with the assurance and confidence that the bounty she hoped for would ever arrive.

Because the Lord did not answer her as the dog and the cat were taken away and the Lord did not answer her now.

It was as if she dwelled in a deep cave.

What else could she do, then, but pray that her words and the words of all the animals of the universe would be heard by somebody, somewhere before it was too late. ✖

Ariel Dorfman is a Chilean-American novelist, playwright, essayist, academic and human rights activist. He was forced into exile in 1973 under Chilean dictator Augusto Pinochet's military coup. He is the author of Death and the Maiden and The Suicide Museum. His latest novel, published in March, is Allegro, a mystery narrated by Mozart

Remember the past to save the future

SARAH DAWOOD introduces two poems by **DIANE FAHEY**, which use the power of verse to remind us of historical stories of persecution that we must never forget

ABOVE: Diane Fahey's poem The Hands focuses on the resounding impact of imperialism

AS WE WITNESS the rise of far-right movements around the world and a shift away from tolerance, Australian poet Diane Fahey's two poems featured here speak to frightening and unpredictable times. But they also explore how hope comes from standing up to hatred, and how art can be a powerful tool to do this.

Fahey, who was born in Melbourne and still lives in the state of Victoria, has had a decorated career and is the author of 13 poetry collections. She typically focuses on landscape and the natural world, Greek myths, fairy tales and visual art. It is interesting, then, that these two poems are of a political and historical nature and broach "subjects I would ordinarily not presume to take on in my work as a poet," she told Index.

These works explore the complex topics of imperialism (The Hands) and antisemitism (The Fix), and were initially inspired by "two small but powerful personal memories", based on conversations with individuals who have experienced the impacts of these issues in India and Europe respectively.

Fahey felt it was important to use her voice to "remember" the disturbing events of the past, at a time when the world is increasingly overcome with attempts to erase the truth through the weaponised use of disinformation and the unstoppable spread of misinformation online.

"One force working against remembrance, and the sense of connection it brings, is the relentless attack on facts in many societies now," she said. "The human mind blindsiding itself to the destructiveness of hatred and racism as it existed then, as it exists now."

Indeed, art in all its forms can be used to recall horrendous acts, and therefore increase our compassion for others. Quoting the author Elif Shafak, Fahey said: "Stories bring us together, untold stories keep us apart".

The Hands, which depicts the brutal effects of colonialism in both ancient and modern-day civilisations, showcases the hand as a symbol of personal agency. It begins with hand-holding, a representation of friendship, and ends with hands being severed by a blade, a representation of unprovoked extreme violence. Hands make art, offer help, enable citizens to vote, but also commit murder, enact abuse, and demonstrate obedience to tyranny, such as through the Nazi salute.

Personal agency, when used positively, can be used to support others or for self-discovery. In The Fix, music is used to demonstrate this, and show how the artform can have healing powers to tackle inner hatred, resentment and fears of the other. If allowed to build up with no outlet, internalised feelings can "become toxic and lead to the projection of blame onto others", Fahey said.

Art, alongside news reporting and academia, can form part of the rich tapestry of storytelling that ensures persecution, oppression and ethnic cleansing are not forgotten. Many may shy away from such topics, either because they feel powerless, uninformed, or simply that they find them too painful, Fahey said. But in exploring the past and present, we seek a better future.

"Every act by which we increase our awareness and understanding of the victims of these great tragedies can, I believe, deepen empathy and therefore take us further along the path of seeking creative, non-violent solutions to conflict and division," she said.

Sarah Dawood is editor at Index on Censorship

Diane Fahey is an Australian poet who has produced 13 poetry collections. She has won multiple awards, including the 1985 Mattara Poetry Prize and the 1987 Wesley Michel Wright Prize, and has been published internationally. She holds a PhD in creative writing from the University of Western Sydney →

The Hands

by DIANE FAHEY

The Strongest Poison ever known
Came from Caesar's Laurel Crown
– William Blake, Auguries of Innocence

I remember them, decades ago
at a conference – two young women

in shining saris, both beautiful,
devoted friends holding hands.

One said: "Before the British came,
India was a rich country."

They gave me, in return for
a book they may not have wanted,

a bracelet of malachite beads
that I still have, will wear one day.

*

I'm getting old, time to be direct
and, if possible, brief.

This, as I understand it,
is the mindset of those who

take, or take over,
as if by right,

territory, whole countries
and their material resources,

extracting, too, the freedom of lives,
the strength of bodies, their work-power,

while crushing where they can
the living spirit of a culture,

its precepts of honour and value,
its sacred beliefs:

We'll come and take the best of what you have
then turn the best of what you are

into liabilities
so as to feed and further our desire for

ascendancy –
on multiple fronts, in every conceivable way.

Thus we will plant the seeds of
internalised oppression –

a labyrinth some may become lost in
while others defy, resist.

So there will be, of course,
actual slaughter – why deny it?

The stories fill so many books.
And we shall never be sated –

even after the long decline, the fall,
we'll leave our mark.

*

When the Romans were leaving Britain,
some soldiers cut off, as they passed,

hands of townspeople and villagers –
because they could,

ruining lives on a whim.
Old Imperialism ends –

some vicious fool's greedy dream
of power and blood and gold.

New Imperialism starts,
likewise spawning war, mayhem,

measureless human grief.
All this is played out, daily,

in live reportage, print and image.
Daily, I wish it were not so.

The Fix

by DIANE FAHEY

1
In some parts of Europe
the music of Felix Mendelssohn,
a Jew,
is never performed

even in these times
(especially in these times?) –

so a visitor to my country,
a great pianist in old age,
mentioned between playing pieces
wherein his fingers summoned

the burdensome, often savage
difficulty, and the hope –
that famous crack filled with raw, searing daylight –
of the human estate

as known and grappled with
by Beethoven, Schubert, Brahms,
by Felix and his sister Fanny
and by the many others

whose music can be, if we so choose,
a stream running through our days –
offering the balm of renewal,
inviting acceptance of
the universal fact of suffering.

2
Adolf Hitler's private library
contained many books and tracts
lauding antisemitism –

a manoeuvre, a ploy,
embedded in the mind-life of
Europe (and wherever).

We know what flames he was fuelling.

3
It can be so hard to stand in the light –
the light of our days in this world –
and lay claim to our life
as it has been given to us –
to shape and nurture it, and if need be,
to mend, seek a better way.

Why not a worse way? –
so a hidden voice may prompt.
Blame and scapegoat
then fit yourself up as the victim –

the victim of life, of history,
of economics, of "them"
(who? – multiple-choice question,
fill in the blank space as you wish).

Life, a multiple-choice question.

Notes for The Fix:
1) I remember clearly the remark alluded to at the beginning of The Fix, heard in a radio broadcast of a Musica Viva piano recital in 2018, but did not hear the name of the artist – but it was almost certainly Hungarian-British classical pianist Sir András Schiff. An article by him regarding how underrated Mendelssohn's music is can be found at: oae.co.uk/the-underrated-giant/
2) Richard Wagner, a hostile critic of Mendelssohn and his music due to his "Jewishness", described his death at the age of 42 in 1847 as "… the death that Mendelssohn's guardian angel sealed at the right time by closing his eyes permanently." – Forbidden Music. The Jewish Composers Banned by the Nazis, by Michael Haas, p.32. (Yale University Press, 2013).
3) "There is a crack in everything, that's how the light gets in," is a line from the song Anthem by Leonard Cohen.
4) Peter Hughes, a broadcaster with a PhD in philosophy, wrote: "When being is a crime, it collectivises guilt and offers a totalising explanation of malevolence… If we are to counter hate and prejudice, there can be no preference in suffering. The philosopher Arthur Schopenhauer wrote that 'misfortune in general is the rule'. He believed that acknowledging universal suffering 'makes us see other men in a true light and reminds us of what are the most necessary of all things: tolerance, patience, forbearance and charity, which each of us needs and which each of us therefore owes'".
aspectsofhistory.com/antisemitism-and-the-statue-of-mendelssohn ✖

Where it's more dangerous to carry a camera than a gun

ANTONIA LANGFORD speaks to a Yemeni cinematographer who found inspiration in a displaced singer, and was determined to record joy inside one of the world's biggest humanitarian crises

ABOVE: Scenes from the film Fariha, where young filmmakers put themselves at risk to show the joy of music

EVERY DETAIL IS captured fondly by the lens. The kiosk, a whimsical farrago of vividly colourful scarves, dusty packaged goods and glittery tinsel. The sun passing gently over the woman's animated features as she sings.

"Sure, my voice is nice. Even if it weren't, I can always add some sugar to sweeten it," she giggles.

It is a visual language of love. But for Dheya al-Mandi, a 27-year-old cinematographer from Yemen, it is also a forbidden language.

"In my city Sana'a, if you hold a camera, it is more dangerous than if you hold a gun," al-Mandi said. He recalled how even children would scatter in fear when they saw him carrying his filming equipment, and how Houthi soldiers accused him of being a spy for Saudi Arabia or the USA.

"To them, if you hold a gun, you're a good person, a normal person. But if they see you holding a camera, that's when they ask you why you are shooting."

Film is a gift al-Mandi has nurtured since early childhood even when means were scarce. As a teenager, he started shooting pictures on his phone and noticed he had a talent for framing beautiful shots and observing small details.

The dreams he grew up with were burdened by war, loss and despair: since 2014, Yemen has been engulfed in a devastating civil war marked for many people by near-constant displacement and famine. The conflict is often called one of the world's worst humanitarian crises.

Most of Yemen's northern highlands and the capital, Sana'a, are controlled by the Iran-backed Houthi movement – also known as Ansar Allah – an armed rebel group made up of mostly Zaidi Shia Muslims. Yemen's internationally-recognised government controls much of the south and east of the country. Longstanding conflict between the Houthis and the Saudi Arabian-backed government has left more than half of the country's population in desperate need of humanitarian assistance.

But if anything, al-Mandi said, adversity only made his dreams loftier.

"When you make art in a place which is not safe, it is more special than when you do it in a place of sanctuary," he said. "People living in dangerous places – we still love to sing, to dance, and we do it with all these consequences and difficulties facing us. It becomes more beautiful."

This is the subject of the 2024 half-hour documentary he worked on, Fariha, directed by Badr Yousef. Fariha follows the story of its eponymous heroine, Fariha Hassan, once a well-known Yemeni singer from the coastal city of Hodeidah.

Hassan abandoned her successful career decades ago, disillusioned with the lack of support and respect for artists and repressive cultural attitudes towards female performers. Displaced from her city and now in her seventies, Hassan has returned to singing on the street and in her kiosk in Sana'a, where the director Yousef discovered her surrounded by curious passers-by and admirers. The film tracks her aspiration to return to the stage once more.

"I am Fariha, and I make people happy with my songs," is her sunny introduction. It is easy to see how the team of filmmakers fixed on her as a subject. She is bright, defiant and passionate. She is also flamboyant and expressive, wearing an eclectic mixture of fabrics and prints, gesturing and emoting theatrically. Her name means joy.

He promised as a condition of his release that he would never hold a camera again

Hassan was discovered in the 1980s, whilst working as a hospital janitor. She would while away the hours singing as she cleaned, her powerful voice reverberating in the long corridors. It didn't take long for her to be noticed, and she was invited to join the band of the well-known pioneering Yemeni singer Nabat Ahmed, with whom she toured. Hassan then became well-established in her own right, later recording albums alone.

Decades later, her voice is as strong and versatile as it was then, modulating effortlessly between soaring belts and softer, fluttering melodies. She sings Yemeni traditional songs, but also improvisations, her hands ghosting swiftly across the *tabla* drums she sometimes uses for percussion. With no musical education, her ability is instinctive, almost mystical.

Capturing Hassan's unbreakable spirit meant two years of intimate involvement in her life, tracking every moment closely with the camera. Al-Mandi and the director recorded her on the streets, at her work, in the kitchen enjoying quiet moments with her beloved cat Sudy. On one occasion, the camera was rolling as she happened upon a lover from decades ago in the street who had also been displaced from her city, capturing the tears of their long-awaited reunion.

"In documentary, the most important thing is that you film everything," al-Mandi said. "You have to show every detail, every interruption. The interruptions build the story."

Some interruptions were less welcome. One day, filming with Hassan in the labyrinthine streets of the Old City, they were approached by Houthi rebels and detained. Unbeknownst to their captors, the camera and microphones were still recording, capturing the entire ordeal. Al-Mandi said he promised as a condition of his release that he would never hold a camera again.

"The Houthis are afraid of the media and the news, they don't want people to see how we really live in Yemen," he said. "But filming is my dream. Why should I leave it because of your war?"

In some ways, the young filmmakers

ABOVE: Fariha Hassan has had her return to music documented after she was displaced from her home in Hodeidah

al-Mandi and Yousef found in Hassan a mirror of their own conflict, between passion and repression. Her transgressive determination to sing in public despite stigma and intimidation, al-Mandi said, inspired his own decision to keep pursuing film. Since filming finished, everyone involved in the project has fled the country. Al-Mandi has sought asylum in the UK.

The filmmakers also found hope that one day the rich visual and musical cultures of Yemen might be encouraged to thrive. Hassan, al-Mandi said, is a role model for people in Yemen, encouraging them to keep making art even when adversity seems overwhelming.

"Even people living in a place of war want to see the art of their country," he said. "The beauty of the streets, the artists, the emotions and feelings of the people, how they love each other, how they could live in peace. That's why I want to tell the truth of this place." ✖

Antonia Langford is a freelance journalist who writes for publications including The Guardian, The i Paper and The New European

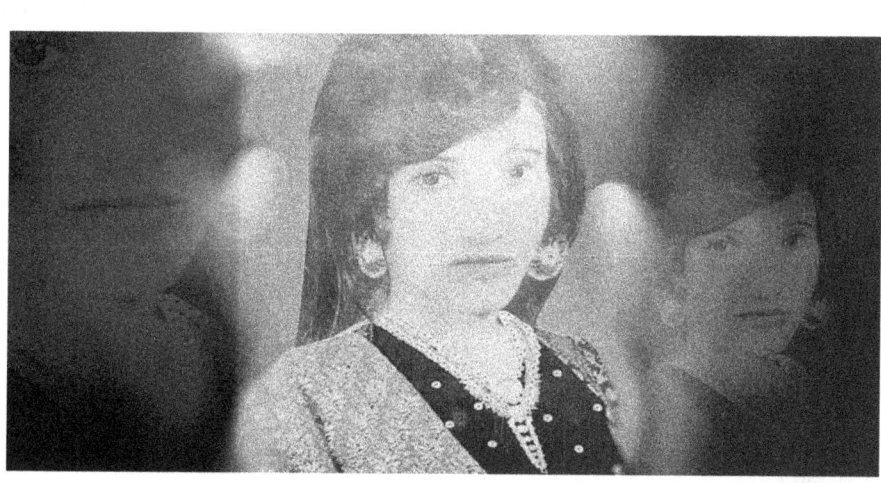

ABOVE: Now in her seventies, Fariha Hassan was a popular singer in the 1980s

LAST WORD

The fight for change isn't straightforward

Award-winning disability inclusion specialist **SHANI DHANDA** has dedicated her career to combatting social inequality

ABOVE: "It's frustrating that other people's assumptions about me impact my life outcomes," says Shani Dhanda

SHANI DHANDA SET up the Asian Woman Festival, the Asian Disability Network and the UK's Diversability Card, a discount card for disabled people. In 2020, she was included on the BBC's 100 Women list.

She speaks to Index about her journey into activism and her view of the new Trumpian world order.

INDEX What made you embrace activism?

DHANDA As a South Asian disabled woman from a working-class background, I've had to deal with a kind of exclusion that's shaped pretty much everything about my life. There's this constant feeling of being over excluded or underestimated, not just because of my health condition [a bone condition called osteogenesis imperfecta], but because of where I'm from and who I am. These overlapping parts of my identity shape how others view me, often limiting my potential before they even give me a shot. It's frustrating that other people's assumptions about me impact my life outcomes. That's what pushed me to become an activist.

INDEX How have attitudes to disability changed in Britain since you were a child?

DHANDA Some improvements have been made, but many places remain inaccessible; transport is still not accessible and buildings often lack ramps or lifts. However, it's the negative attitudes towards disabled people that remain the most stubborn barrier. When it comes to employment, ableism is still a huge issue. Disabled people are twice as likely to be unemployed and cuts to social care continue to hit us the hardest.

INDEX How can marginalised groups get their voices heard?

DHANDA By being clear about what they're trying to achieve – whether that's better access to healthcare, more representation or real change in policy. Organising through community-led advocacy, using social media to amplify their messages, and partnering with allies in healthcare and policy can make a huge difference.

INDEX How do you feel about the executive orders on diversity, equity and inclusion (DEI) Donald Trump made on entering office?

DHANDA For me, it was a reminder that the fight for real change isn't always straightforward and it felt like it would set back our progress. But it also made me feel more determined. It pushed people to speak up and take action, proving that we're not backing down from fighting for fairness and inclusion no matter how much resistance there is.

INDEX Others now seem to feel empowered to persecute women, people of colour and disabled people. Will people still speak out?

DHANDA I don't always feel supported in those moments. As a broadcaster I regularly get trolled. First, they'll target my disability, then my race, ethnicity and nationality and, if they get to it, maybe my gender. It's like there's this constant pressure to stay quiet because speaking up often feels like it just brings more hate. But, despite that, I keep pushing; the more we speak the more we stand a chance of changing things.

INDEX If you were jailed for your activism, which book would you take with you?

DHANDA But What Will People Say? Navigating Mental Health, Identity, Love and Family Between Cultures by Sahaj Kaur Kohli.

INDEX Which piece of art has inspired or moved you most?

DHANDA The Revolution Will Not Be Televised, by Gil Scott-Heron.

INDEX Which news headline would you be happiest to read?

DHANDA "Intersectional inclusion legalised globally: A new era of equity for all". ✖

Shani Dhanda is an inclusion accessibility specialist and broadcaster. Follow her at @ShaniDhanda

www.ingramcontent.com/pod-product-compliance
Lightning Source LLC
Chambersburg PA
CBHW080215040426
42333CB00044B/2688